Watching God set people free is a deep passion fo
the privilege of watching her lovingly lead people in times of prayer that have
resulted in breakthrough moments in their lives. I am thrilled she has poured her
heart and experience into *First Freedoms*. I have no doubt all who read this will
be inspired and challenged to cultivate a deeper prayer life and walk with Jesus.

Dr. Darren Whitehead, senior pastor, Church of the City, Franklin, TN

There are some books that are meant to be read, and other books that are meant
to be absorbed. *First Freedoms* falls in the latter category. It is both inspiration-
al and instructional. It is deeply profound yet wonderfully practical. Whether
you are a longtime follower of Jesus hungry to grow your friendship with God,
a struggling Christian trying to connect with a God who seems distant, or a
curious seeker in search of more, this book is for you. My life, ministry, and
church family have been forever shaped and blessed by the realities that Jen puts
forth in this book, and I am grateful that blessing is now available to you as well.

Dave Clayton, author of *Revival Starts Here* and pastor at
Ethos Church, Nashville, TN

First Freedoms is the book every church leader should be fighting for and knows
they need but has never had packaged like this. It's a beautiful thing to watch
my friend Jennifer do what Jesus said and unite the church under a banner of
freedom. She's doing it one prayer at a time, and every ministry leader needs to
work through this book.

Rachel Faulkner Brown, director of Be Still Ministries
and Never Alone Widows

In my experiences with both new and experienced Christians over the years, I've
witnessed a disturbingly profound disconnect between the heart of the believer
and the heart of God, accompanied by a growing despair that there should be
so much more. Jennifer Barnett courageously leaps right into the heart of this
chasm like an experienced bridge-builder, offering accessible tools to believers
that invite them into the very heart of God, one relational step at a time. *First
Freedoms* is so much more than a book to be consumed; it is an invitation to
every believer, at any stage of their journey, to experience the relational fullness,
freedom, and fruitfulness of the Father, Son, and Spirit.

Rob Touchstone, director of Business as Mission at Lipscomb
University and cofounder of The Well Coffeehouse

I have listened to my dear friend and ministry partner, Jennifer, teach various topics in our Freedom Prayer trainings, and often thought, *Man I wish that was written down somewhere. It's so good!* Well, now it is. And we all are the beneficiaries of her insights and applications. I highly recommend you take your time with *First Freedoms*, both alone and with others. It will be transformational.

Andy Reese, author and president of Freedom Prayer

Every page of this book is worth reading. Each one contributes to unlocking the wonderful freedom that Jesus wants us to experience. I would consider its principles to be one of the main reasons CrossBridge is such an emotionally healthy and spiritually powerful church. This book is full of hope!

Kirk Freeman, lead pastor of CrossBridge Community Church, San Antonio, TX

Working in a crisis center, I hear an amplification of our culture's question: Where is hope for freedom from wounds and lies and sin and all the outworkings of evil that wreck our lives and the lives around us? Far from trying to find this hope in ourselves, our own insights, and our own behavior modification, *First Freedoms* offers a refreshing guide to the practices of Jesus that open us up to intimacy with God so he can bring about real freedom. The pages of this book throw open wide the door to hope and offer an attunement to hear the voice of the One who beckons us to enter.

Adam Graham, LPC and MHSP, director of emergency psychiatric services

JENNIFER BARNETT

FIRST FREEDOMS

Drawing Near to God by Cultivating a
Wholehearted Prayer Life

Nashville, Tennessee

*To the many people
who have bravely taken those
first steps in Freedom Prayer.*

CONTENTS

ACKNOWLEDGEMENTS

I want to thank my beloved Ethos family, CrossBridge Freedom Groups, and the Freedom Prayer teams in Evansville, Indiana, and Tucson, Arizona, for the trial run of this devotional. Much love to Lauren, Caity, and the Jeannies for your wisdom, edits, and intercession. I'm grateful for Andy, who taught me to walk and who cheers me on as I run, and I'm thankful for my parents, who pray for every race. Finally, thank you, Cory, as you patiently help me train and delight when I decide to sprint. You are my most treasured running buddy.

INTRODUCTION

Have you ever watched a young child learn to walk? Their shaky first steps—often taken in the presence of the smiles and outstretched hands of a parent poised to catch them—are exhilarating to watch. Taking those steps becomes the single focus of the child's family for a season. Getting those steps secure by practicing them over and over again becomes the household mission. The family cheers and counts and coaxes.

We all understand just how important those first steps are for a child and how foundational they are for their next steps in life. No one expects a young child to take their first few steps and immediately break into a run or skip or cartwheel. We know that wobbly steps mature into more confident steps. We also know that children must have time to grow in walking before they can access more complex movements.

I have watched my children grow from those first few baby steps, and now they are experiencing new "firsts" in their teenage years. My fifteen-year-old is learning how to drive a car, which is testing everything I thought I knew about parenting, patience, trust, geometry, and the law. The law wisely requires a teenager first to drive with a permit and get help from a trusted adult who guides them along the way. Parents sensibly enroll their teenagers in a driver's education class, which provides space to "build up" from driving in a neighborhood cul-de-sac to navigating a busy interstate.

> *We know that wobbly steps mature into more confident steps.*

Parents are not *controlling* because they enforce the law's limits on their young driver. Instead, they are offering a grace to their child by allowing them to practice those first steps of driving safely, over and over again, before changing the scenario. Parents want a process that's both comfortable and repetitive before the conditions become challenging—all in order to seek their child's success.

In the same manner, I've written this book about "first freedoms" with the intention that you would practice these firsts over and over again, until it becomes natural for you to live in them. These first freedoms come from Scripture and include learning to abide with God and intentionally allowing him to search your heart for anything that blocks your communion with him. They are good for you and contribute to your spiritual growth. These first freedoms are foundational in the Christian journey and are meant to be practiced again and again with great joy and anticipation, much like a baby's first steps and a teenager's first drive behind the wheel. They are pillars of personal sanctification, and they can help us develop a wholehearted prayer life near to God. He gives them to us as our first steps and desires to give us other consequent experiences as a result of our initial experiences in these truths. They are necessary for our growth and liberty in Christ.

Yet sadly Christians often completely skim or bypass them in their personal discipleship. I have had the privilege of praying with thousands of mature Christian believers who were never taught these first freedoms. They limped through the Christian life due to a less than ideal start: at conversion they took a few toddler steps and then immediately were expected to do backflips as they jumped into service, mission, and ministry. They did not experience a safe environment to learn and practice how to grow into these important disciplines in prayer. They weren't cheered on during their first spiritual steps, and they didn't receive necessary assistance before they made their first turn in busy traffic. They charged into the Christian life without even having practiced these freedoms. For some, they never experienced them at all. I have watched too many twenty-somethings become spiritually burnt out, disillusioned, or just done with God, simply because they sprinted out of the gate after their new birth. They started out fast, but later confess:

> They never learned to walk with him before they tried to run with him.

I have observed older adults who continue showing up to church and small groups, yet they are bitter, disappointed, and grieved about their relationship with God. They wonder if a relationship with God is really worth it: *Is he even there? Can I even gain access to him?* They limp through the "right things" but know deep down that they were made to run, even though they have not really taken their first steps. They long to run the race, but they struggle at the end of the day just to put one foot in front of the other. The resulting shame and condemnation of not being able to move in the way that they know they should—the way that Scripture describes—leaves them guilty and discouraged. God holds an abundance of grace, waiting for them to draw near.

If you relate to these examples, then take heart: there exists abundant grace for you too. No matter how long you've tried to sprint with broken feet or on rocky foundations, it's never too late to begin learning those first steps anew. God invites both new and seasoned believers to "stand at the crossroads and look; ask for the ancient paths, ask where the good way is, and walk in it, and you will find rest for your souls" (Jer. 6:16). God does not intend for us to limp through our spiritual life without strengthened and solid muscles.

First Freedoms can provide both restoration and routine to your prayer life in order to strengthen your race-ready legs. And it's those first steps in prayer that really matter. We never waste time learning them, practicing them, and working to steady them. These freedoms strengthen and stretch legs ready to run spiritual marathons. They are not a means to an end; they are the beginning, middle, and end of a healthy prayer life. Most importantly, they are the foundation on which everything is built.

As you read through this book, you'll have the opportunity to grow in these freedoms we have in Christ: drawing near to God, abiding continually in him, forgiving from the heart, exchanging lies for the truth, engaging in spiritual warfare, holding on to anchors in suffering, practicing holy authority, and more.

My hope is that you cherish these first freedoms and find holy joy in walking them out. Much like the loving parent who reaches for their wobbly toddler with no expectations other than experiencing that milestone with their child, our good Father reaches toward us in delight. He sees us as his sons and daughters and wants to help us learn to walk with him and through him and for him. God has always been about relationship in our Christian journey, and these first freedoms are vital for that bond to hold secure. So don't despise the shaky legs; they can become strong in trust and faith. Along this journey, in the midst of the wobbly steps, God reaches out his hand and waits for you.

HOW TO USE THIS STUDY

You can easily use this study as an individual or within a group context. Ideally, you will experience it in both ways. As such, each chapter contains "Personal Prayer" and "Community Connection" sections, which contain exercises and questions for your use.

For Individuals. As you work through the study as an individual, I recommend that you take one week with each chapter to practice the steps in the Personal Prayer sections. Because the Personal Prayer practices are foundational to the Christian walk, it is not only okay, but I actually encourage you to repeat the practices for several days as part of your daily conversation with God. This will help you become comfortable with them in your prayer life. Even if you're going through this study purely on your own, you can use the Community Connection questions as well—praying through them individually instead of within a group.

For Groups. If you are working through this study with a small group or in a Bible study context, I recommend you practice and respond to the Personal Prayer section throughout the week on your own and arrive at your group's meeting with questions and specific pieces from that section that impacted you. Then when you come together as a group, use the group time to work through any difficulties or successes that might have occurred in the Personal Prayer section during the week. As time allows, move on to the Community Connection questions as a group, recognizing that there is overlap between the Personal Prayer and Community Connection sections. The topics in both sections are personal and center on each person's unique interactions with the Lord.

If you are working as a group, the number of participants typically ranges from four to ten, so that everyone has space to participate in the Community Connection section. While some larger Bible study groups can study *First Freedoms* corporately, I recommend these larger groups branch into smaller groups of ten or fewer for the Community Connection discussions.

As you go through this devotional, keep in mind you need not complete all of the items each week in the Community Connection section. You can select the questions from that section that are most relevant to your group discussion. The most important encouragement I will give you is this: engage with your group transparently and in unity, focusing on the goal of encountering God together.

Depending on how much time you permit for the meetings, the moderator or leader can select beforehand only certain items from each section for your group to pray through or discuss. A designated leader is not necessary if you're simply using *First Freedoms* as a book study outside of an organized church gathering, but someone will need to at least guide the discussions and decide on questions to meet the group's needs each week. They can do this by asking group members to suggest the questions that are pertinent to their particular interests.

EXTENDING GRACE TO ONE ANOTHER

It is important for everyone in the group to remember that each individual has a unique relationship with God, and that everyone's prayer life is deeply personal. This means each person will naturally lean toward their own spiritual wiring during prayer, and this is okay. For example, if someone is wired to *feel* more easily, they may speak about the Personal Prayer pieces using "sensing" language. They might comment, "I sensed God's presence near me and felt that he wanted me to know this . . ." If someone is wired to *visualize* more easily, they might talk about their prayer experience using word pictures or "seeing" language. If someone loves to *speak*, they might talk in metaphors or use poetic language: "I had fallen into a pit of self-pity and God's grace was the rope to climb out in that moment." These can all be okay, as long as they are biblically sound and match the character of God. The tools in this book lean heavily on Scripture, so leaders may want to set the expectation early that the Word of God is the litmus test for our responses in prayer.

In a group setting, you might face the temptation to compare one way of encountering God to another. Please, don't do that! God related to his children in a variety of ways in the Bible, and we can assume that he continues to do that now. The variety of ways he reveals himself shows how amazing he is! So reject the impulse to compare either by elevating your way of hearing from God *or by diminishing* how he communicates with you, and then extend the same grace to others.

The beauty of a unified group is that each person in the group can see diversity in the glory of God expressed through varied individuals. Group members who are willing to build up and encourage each other in their personal walk are vital, no matter how different their individual ways are of hearing and seeing God. We can all learn from one another and see the imprint of God on the lives of our friends. As we see the Lord specifically respond to his children's needs, we also see God exhort us to greater intimacy and lead us even to a place of worship.

Recognizing this beauty can help us see a greater representation of his character and personality in the specific way he responds to each of us. We see glory in this when we view our differences, not from a comparison lens, but from a lens of appreciation in which we see intimate communion with God as a display of God's vast creativity. So as you begin this study, please give yourself and those with you time and grace to encounter him.

As I've prayed through this material with many individuals, I've found that human nature and fear often tempt us to quit even before we've really begun. The first time we wait and try to hear God we're tempted to give up if we don't encounter him after eight seconds or less, believing that he is not interested in hearing from us or that we are not "gifted" enough to hear him. We feel let down by God and disappointed in ourselves. Yet like most "firsts," it takes time and practice to learn to discern the voice of God from our own thoughts or the enemy's lies; it takes time to expand our expectations past our previous experiences and intentionally hunger to hear the voice of God beyond what we might have previously known; and it takes time to discover the vast ways in which he speaks. Once we've taken time doing so, we even discover that the method through which he speaks can change, depending on what he wants to show us at any given moment.

> *It takes time and practice to learn to discern the voice of God.*

For example, you may recall in prayer a Scripture that you had not thought about in years. It could come back to your mind as you're trying to hear the best next step in an important financial decision. Or you may see a picture in your mind when asking the Lord to show you how he felt about you when you experienced that traumatic childhood experience. Or you may notice a nudge toward a decision that feels like his still small voice directing you. You may even feel his tangible presence as you praise him in prayer. Further still, you may recall a memory when asking for guidance about a significant relationship, and you finally understand that the memory has you stuck and keeps you resorting to old patterns and unhealthy defense mechanisms in the relationship. No matter how he speaks, remember this: you were made to hear God.

His voice is never hurried or frantic but will always align with the fruit of his Spirit (Hab. 2:3; Luke 12:22–26; 1 Kings 19:12). His voice will be peaceful even in instruction and loving even in discipline. He can direct us in a tough impending decision without demonstrating the least bit of stress or worry. While he may require fast obedience, he isn't worried about things falling apart—because he isn't hurried. And he doesn't need to be pushy or domineering to garner a response from us. He is relaxed and resigned in his guidance.

CLEARING THE PATH TOWARD GOD

As you begin to practice hearing from him through *First Freedoms*, your first prayer time or two might feel awkward and a bit like work. That is completely normal. It's like when my oldest son has to clear the path in the woods behind our home. He likes to go hiking on the trails but has to climb a big hill to get there. From the time that winter moves into spring, those trails that were stark and bare become overgrown with vines, weeds, and small trees that begin to grow seemingly overnight. So when he heads out to conquer the hill at the beginning of summer, he doesn't get very far without pausing to chop, cut, and clear brush and branches.

He has learned to take all sorts of hiking knives and garden clippers to do the job. It is hard work, but the next day as he goes hiking through the trails again, the path is fairly clear. While the previous day required all sorts of equipment, now he can even walk the path with us as a family. In fact, we laugh as we watch our son head up the hill the next day with simply a plastic sword to swat away spider webs, which are the only things that "grew" since the previous day of chopping and cutting. Day after day, as he walks the trail, the path becomes more worn with a clearer way to the top.

In the same way, the time we spend "clearing the path" at the beginning of our journey pays off as we seek the Lord and learn to commune with him in prayer. Our daily walk with him along the trails becomes clearer and our steps easier. I hope and pray *First Freedoms* helps clear those trails that lead you toward God again, or perhaps for the first time, so that you can keep walking them during every season of your life.

THE CONNECTION

In order to cultivate a wholehearted prayer life,
we must be connected to God. Most of us know we
should be in close relationship with him, but we never
received practical steps on how to actually draw near.
Yet once we take those first steps to connect to God, we
can stay connected and grow in our relationship with
him. In Part 1, we will explore the biblical concepts
of wholeheartedly drawing near to God as Father,
abiding with him, and securing our connection to him
through a healthy prayer life.

COMMUNION WITH GOD

*Search me, God, and know my heart; test me and
know my anxious thoughts. See if there is any offensive
way in me, and lead me in the way everlasting.*

— Psalm 139:23–24

The language in Psalm 139:23–24 has always challenged me and simultaneously beckoned me toward more. It is poetic and beautiful, this idea of God searching and knowing a person's heart, but it is also active and participatory. As I read it, I'm humbled to recognize that the God of the universe has a vested interest in my heart—and in removing from me what is anxious and offensive that clouds my vision. He wants to be near me. He wants my heart to be whole. Despite my blemishes, God wants to lead me in the way everlasting. There is hope for me, and God is close to me in the process.

As you begin the exercises of this study, allow me to share an important assumption of mine, and know that I share this assumption in order to help you feel secure during your pursuit of first freedoms: I assume that you, as a participant in this study, believe you were made for a relationship with God. As part of a complete relationship with him, I also assume you believe you were made to talk to him through prayer and that you believe God communicates back to us as we pray.

Simply said, I assume that you believe on some level you can truly connect with God through prayer, by which we speak to God and he speaks to us. I assume that on some level, you long for a wholehearted prayer life, where you can draw near to God and where you hide nothing before him. That God would have access to every part of your heart, your story, and your history, and that you would trust him with all of it. That you could talk to him, and that he would respond in a way that you understand. Prayer is essentially a conversation with God, and God is not a passive participant in the conversation. So even if you have never experienced God speaking to you, I write with the assumption that you believe and hope for this kind of conversation in prayer.

If you feel that you lack personal experience with this type of communion with God or that you are a bit shaky in your faith in this regard, let me assure you that these are common barriers for those who pursue these freedoms. I find the Lord is generally quick to respond to our desperation and desire. Our spiritual résumés, even though seemingly lacking, are inconsequential to God, who sees our hearts and knows what we need. Communion with God in prayer involves hearing from God and seeing God as we wait for his response. Once we encounter his voice, it is our responsibility to respond back.

HEARING GOD

My belief that Christians can hear from God is rooted in Scripture passages about God's character and desire for relationship. While I know some people believe God no longer speaks to us, I find the argument for that belief to be based on false understandings of Scripture passages and in great contradiction to God's heart for communion with his children. When we observe the way Jesus responded to people in relationship, we gain insight into God's response to us in prayer. Healthy relationships are two-sided, and communication is vital to their health.

> Prayer is a primary means of God's grace to help us encounter the Lord.

In the Garden, we find God walking and talking with Adam and Eve (Gen. 3:8). Throughout the Scriptures, God is with his children—guiding, reproving, and restoring them back to himself. It would be out of character for him as a living and active God to just stop what he has been doing from the beginning. The prophet Jeremiah speaks God's words: "Call to me and I will answer you and tell you great and unsearchable things you do not know"

(Jer. 33:3). God's heart continually seeks to help us grow in communication with him as we depend on him for knowledge and revelation.

In John 10, Jesus says his sheep hear his voice, know it, and follow him. In the context of that passage, it is not only essential to their relationship for the sheep to hear the shepherd but also crucial for the sheep's survival and protection from thieves, liars, wolves—and ultimately from the enemy. Knowing what the Lord's voice sounds like is a non-negotiable for followers of the Good Shepherd. In 1 John 1:3, we read a similar emphasis on not just hearing God, but having fellowship with him: "We proclaim to you what we have seen and heard, so that you also may have fellowship with us. And our fellowship is with the Father and with his Son, Jesus Christ." We have fellowship with God, and by definition, that fellowship is active and happens in the context of a community of people with similar interests and experiences. It would be nearly impossible to have fellowship with another Christian without communion or conversation with them. Like those relationships, our fellowship with God must be ongoing and in the process of continual growth, which requires us to hear from God. On some level, we must be familiar with the voice of God, with spiritual ears tuned to hear him in how he speaks and instructs.

> *God is not a passive participant in prayer.*

SEEING GOD

"Seeing God" is another way to describe our experiences with him. Scripture often uses sensory language for this. I believe God understands both our human weakness and our struggle to communicate personally, especially with someone we cannot fully see. Some argue that we cannot "see" God, using passages such as Exodus 33:20, where God says, "You cannot see my face, for no one may see me and live." But we must take into account that Greek and Hebrew words for "see" in the Bible carry some pretty broad meanings. Here are five to consider.

We can see with the physical eye (*blepōœ* in Greek), but we can also see or "behold in a vision" (*hΩzq* in Hebrew); we can "take heed" and perceive with the mind inwardly (*horaōœ* in Greek), and we can metaphorically see by knowing with the mind (*eidon* in Greek). Then we can consider, discern, or gaze upon God (*r)h* in Hebrew). So while on this side of eternity we cannot *physically* see God, we can "see" him in other ways as these other definitions reveal.

If we could not, why would the psalmist instruct us to, "Look to the LORD and his strength; seek his face always" (Ps. 105:4)? Or what would be the point of 2 Chronicles 7:14: "If my people, who are called by name, will humble themselves and pray and seek my face and turn from their wicked ways, then I will hear from heaven, and I will forgive their sin and will heal their land"? Further, Paul says we see God by continually beholding the Lord's glory as we are transformed into the likeness of Jesus (2 Cor. 3:18).

While we cannot see God in all of his splendor with our physical eyes, he has equipped us with senses and a mind to encounter him. In fact, he wants to own and have access to those "screens" in our mind that are rightfully his, such as the places where our minds can be impressed by a thought, where we can create new ideas, and where we can recall moments from our past. This is what Paul is getting at in Ephesians 1:18: "That the eyes of your heart may be enlightened in order that you may know the hope to which he has called you, the riches of his glorious inheritance." God made us to see him with spiritual eyes and to encounter him in ways that run deeper and truer than what we can physically see.

SENSING GOD

Take stock for a moment of the vast amounts of useless or even life-draining thoughts that float through your "mind's eye"—that space in your mind where you can close your eyes and picture people, places, and interactions. Get to the mental place where you can think about something in the past, such as what you ate for lunch or what you imagine this afternoon will look like in traffic driving home. Consider how all of those faculties—what we think, see, hear, smell, imagine, and feel—are bombarded daily by social media, television, technology, and entertainment. Even worse, consider how we can be bombarded by our own self-promoting and greedy imaginations!

Consider now how God wants to fill the very senses he created. As believers, we have been given "the mind of Christ" (1 Cor. 2:16), with the eyes of our heart made to encounter him. This is not just strictly a cognitive knowledge-based encounter, but a wholehearted one through which we can both see him and hear him with our spiritual eyes and ears. Communion is not just knowing *about him* but *knowing him fully*. If that were not so, his Word would not instruct us to wait on him, seek his face, and know his voice. Since communion is a goal in our relationship with God, then, logically, he wants us to use our minds and senses, which he created, to help us encounter him. Scripture uses sensory words so we can know him fully—not just intellectually but on every level.

If God did not want to commune with us on a sensory level, he would not have used parables and pictures to offer truths. But he did through Jesus. A picture communicates depth and layers that words cannot, and when we read Jesus' parables, we typically can see them in our minds in ways that are personal to us. I have asked many people to "picture" Psalm 23 in prayer, and hearing people describe their variety of responses is beautiful. That psalm shows up on that screen in their mind that can create and imagine, and it is often deeply personal and specific to their life. Thus, God knows how to relay information in ways we can understand by what we see and feel. His messages are personal and often "speak our language," using those screens in our mind to communicate.

Consider another example of a sensory-level approach to experiencing God. Matthew 7:7–8 depicts God's heart for how he wants us to seek him: by knocking on a door that "will be opened." This is not a literal door but a figure of speech. This picture helps us understand who he is, even though our physical eyes don't see a literal door. Our spiritual eyes can more easily understand his promises when they're framed in terms of something relatable. I challenge anyone to read this Scripture without seeing a door in their mind's eye. You can't help but see it!

Often people even see where they are in relationship to that door or where God is or his countenance in response to our knocking. God uses that mental picture to help us fully take in this message about his desire to commune with us. And what kind of God would describe this opening door only to mislead us? He wouldn't give us an image like this to trick us or disappoint us. That would counter the very nature of God in Scripture. He wants to reveal himself, and our response to what he reveals usually demonstrates where we are in relationship with him.

Elsewhere in the Scriptures, God describes himself as a shade from heat, a refuge, and a stronghold. He is the Rock, Banner, and Shield. The metaphors and names used to describe his nature are endless, and they help us encounter him. Jesus was a carpenter by trade, but people more often think of Jesus as the Good Shepherd. Why? Because we find something very inviting about this part of his personality. We can picture a shepherd, and we know that good shepherds tend to their flock and keep them safe. The picture reveals something in God's character that we long for. We can see it and understand.

The many pictures God uses in Scripture to engage our mind's eye prove that he intended for us to use our imaginations to encounter him. For at least this *First Freedoms* study, I hope you are open to the fact that God may want to use the very senses and faculties he created to usher in encounters with him in your prayer life, even if praying in this way is new to you. I know that I want nothing to be off-limits to God in my heart and mind when I go to him in prayer, and I hope you want that too. That way he can have access to the places in our minds where we create, remember, are impressed by, and have an emotional response to him in order to speak to us fully.

We must be open to this communion and allow him to communicate with full access to our hearts and minds in whichever way he pleases. We cannot have the mind of Christ (1 Cor. 2:16) if we only encounter him with just a portion of what he created. We give him permission to communicate, with access to every part and a desire for him to fill it. We find him when we give him full ownership of every place in our heart (Jer. 29:13). That's what a whole-hearted prayer life looks like.

SEEKING SAFE COMMUNION WITH GOD

When we acknowledge that the Lord wants to communicate with us as we pray, then looking at parameters in communion with God is an important next step. Even in our weaknesses, God intends for us to communicate back with him. Of course, God is trustworthy and perfect, but we are flawed and can mishear him at times. Therefore, knowing the boundaries of interacting with God is important. We can hold to these parameters as safe and biblical boundaries as we learn to encounter him more. They give guideposts and offer plenty of grace in the process of growing in prayer, and they also stand as clear markers to know what is and isn't of God.

> *1. His voice aligns with his Word.* God will not say, do, or reveal anything contrary to his Word. Whatever we hear in his still small voice or sense in his presence or even see in our mind's eye—it must

line up with his Word, his character, and his nature to be verified as his voice. Scripture is the manual that depicts who God is, and for him to depart from it would run counter to his holiness. His ways are unchanging, and the Bible gives truths for us to recognize those ways. What we sense from God as we pray will match who he is in Scripture.

2. We can grow in discerning his voice. We are human, which means we are not perfect, and we are capable of misinterpretation, as I mentioned. There is a biblical precedent for discerning the voice of God in the dialogue between a young Samuel and his mentor, Eli. Samuel responded to Eli, believing that Eli had called him, when in fact God had called him (1 Sam. 3). After Samuel mistook the voice of God three times, Eli told him to respond by saying, "Speak, LORD, for your servant is listening" (v. 9). How encouraging to know we can grow in our discernment of his voice even after missing it! Samuel gave a precedent for the process (success and failure) of knowing God's voice.

3. We must reject other voices in prayer. We, like Jesus, can encounter three voices as we pray: our voice, God's voice, and the enemy's voice. Consider Jesus in the wilderness as he encountered the devil twisting truths using Scripture. Or in the Garden of Gethsemane when Jesus stated, "Not my will, but yours" (Luke 22:42). Or the countless times he simply heard what the Father said, and then obeyed. He was aware of the conflict in what he heard and could discern the source of each voice.

Knowing these three important parameters of prayer is crucial, and they point to why I'm such a big fan of praying in groups of two or three, especially for those learning to hear God for the first time. Praying with others like this is also important for those waiting on God for help in a weighty or confusing matter. We can go forth in prayer this way with full faith that God made us to be led by the Spirit and he also made us to be open-handed—because on our own we can more easily miss God's voice and mess it up too. There is grace as we learn and fine-tune our spiritual ears and eyes, but how helpful it is to learn with mentors and friends who encourage us along the way! The early believers set a precedent in Acts for corporately "[devoting] themselves" (2:42) to prayer, and like every other spiritual discipline, it is sometimes easier to learn with friends.

Communion with anyone involves sharing intimate thoughts and feelings, and genuine prayer is the ultimate example of communion with God. God created us to glorify him and enjoy him, and there's no better way to glorify him and enjoy him than by encountering him through prayer. We glorify him fully when we look to him to fill our need to know him and to be known by him—that we would in him alone be satisfied. Many Christians walk around feeling dismal because they do not experience this gift of delightful communion for which they were made.

We tend to approach God with our sin and our worries without spending much time waiting on him and simply enjoying him. Our personal devotion can often lack worship and space for our eyes to be fixed on Jesus for no other reason than to marvel at his glory. There is no greater joy than to know him and be known by him in prayer, when our spirit is delighted to hear his voice, sense his presence, and see with the eyes of our heart what he offers to us in our deep need to enjoy him.

When our prayer lives feel dismal and without his glory, we often abandon the storehouse available to us in communion with God. We do this out of fear or guilt, often because we believe multiple lies swirling in our heads about how God works and who we are. So we retreat, believing that the grace to grow in prayer does not apply *to us*.

But grace *does* apply to us, and we need him to teach us this truth. We are most fulfilled when we seek and find him. The challenge often, though, is we just don't know practically *how* to seek and find him. In the pages that follow, you will have an opportunity to learn how to do so in drawing near to God.

In each chapter of this book, I offer prompts to help you grow in your prayer life. These come in two sections called "Personal Prayer" and "Community Connection." Each of these sections contains questions and prompts, which move in a specific order and help you progress through the main concepts in each chapter. Take as much time as you need with each question, and I encourage you to revisit them throughout the study as you build your capacity to pray. You can return to these on a regular basis in your own time with the Lord. The Personal Prayer section is for you to work through on your own, and the Community Connection section gives you a way to discuss the chapter within a group setting.

PERSONAL PRAYER

As you begin your first Personal Prayer section in this chapter, I recommend you work through each prompt in order and pause after each one, not only to think about each specific prayer point or action, but more importantly to ask the Lord for his response as you seek him. It is normal and very possible that you may not receive a response from him on every question, but you are building your capacity to be still and wait on him. It has been my experience that he often has much more to communicate than we give him time to. Our waiting is good, no matter the outcome. I suggest spending enough time on each number to grasp the concept and really wait on the Lord for a response before you proceed to the next one.

For most people, the Personal Prayer section each week can be completed in one sitting, but it can take multiple sittings over a few days or even a week if you need more time. Whatever amount of time you spend, I recommend you return to the questions and steps and practice multiple times so that it becomes a part of your daily prayer routine with God. The pace is up to you, but it is most important to learn these foundational practices so you can easily return to them again and again in prayer.

1. Before you begin a conversation with God today, take some intentional time to get comfortable with giving him access to your heart and mind by making sure the screens that you encounter him with are active and accessible. Resist the urge, for a moment, to be overly spiritual in this activity, and just close your eyes and picture something to drink. Record in as much detail as you can what you see, describing every part of the scene in your mind.

_____

_____

_____

_____

2. It is likely that you "saw" a very specific drink in a very specific container, possibly free-floating in the air or sitting on a known table in your home. Now read Psalm 23:1–3 and close your eyes. Picture the images of this psalm on the same screen in your mind, inviting the Lord to meet you in it. See the invitation in these verses, feel it, and listen to God. Again, when you are ready, record in as much detail as possible whatever you might have seen, felt, and heard.

_____

_____

_____

_____

_____

_____

_____

3. You likely not only saw in your mind's eye the visuals of Psalm 23 but had an emotional response to it as well. Similar to remembering a treasured birthday party that you loved, you not only saw the image but sensed it and had a response to it emotionally too.

Now close your eyes again in a posture of prayer and ask the Lord if he will allow you to recall a recent situation in your life where you needed to let him restore your soul but you did not go to him. Take stock of how that situation made you feel by simply applying his truth to it using Psalm 23:1–3. Ask the Lord to show you or give you a sense of what it would look like to allow him access to this situation in a place of "leading you beside still waters" and "restoring your soul."

Give yourself some time to see it, feel it, and sense it, listening and waiting for whatever he wants to reveal. Record any details that you sense as you wait on him, knowing that it's okay not to receive great detail—there is peace in the simple and obedient act of waiting on him. We will learn in the weeks to come practical tools to help you see and hear him more.

_____

_____

_____

_____

_____

_____

COMMUNITY CONNECTION

As you begin the Community Connection section here and in each chapter, the goal is to connect with both God and the others in your group. While some discussion is necessary, prioritize time to pray for one another in each meeting. Select a group leader or facilitator if one is not already in place.

In some group meetings, it may be helpful to wait on the Lord in a place of intercession as the group facilitator or leader responds to one or two people to help them inquire of the Lord for further wisdom or places of freedom. You are never a bystander, but part of an intercessory community. If the leader is helping a group member navigate through something in the prompts, begin to silently pray as they assist them. The group leader can also pray out loud if a question requires the group to inquire of the Lord. The other group members can listen quietly, and then share as directed by the leader.

There is freedom for the group to navigate this section based on the group needs or specific areas of interest or inquiry. Ideally in each meeting everyone will participate by sharing, praying, interceding, or exhorting. Each participant should resist the urge to give advice but instead focus on praying and asking the Lord to bring wisdom and counsel. If possible, allow time for every group member to participate at least once in answering a question or praying. Your group's connection with God will only bring greater connection with one another.

1. Begin by sharing with your group your personal responses to seeing as you read Psalm 23 in the Personal Prayer section. Take notice of how the same passage of Scripture can play out on the screen of the mind so differently from person to person, yet still remain so unwaveringly true. How did God show his personal understanding of each person in what he revealed?

2. Knowing that relationship with God is both intimate and personal, and that he has access to our faculties that he created for communion, discuss the pitfalls of quickly reading Scripture without inviting the Lord to meet you as you read his Word. When our time in Scripture is purely cognitive, which easily happens in fast reading, we do not allow him to access the other places that he created in us. What do we miss? How does this affect our concept of prayer?

3. As a group, define what the three voices mentioned in this chapter sound like: the voice of God, the voice of the enemy, and your own will. How do you determine which one is speaking, so you can know how to respond to it?

4. Conclude your group time by praying for one another in the area of growing in greater ability to see and hear God. Pray for specific requests or concerns for each member, such as, "I'm not able to hear him," or, "My imagination is so active. I'm scared to give him access to that part of my mind." Declare as a group your desire that he grow you in your ability to encounter him.

It is freeing and a bit daunting to really ask God to open the eyes of your heart and your spiritual ears to know him more. You can declare that you were made to commune with him, and that you desire to know him fully. Nothing is off-limits when it comes to allowing God to search your heart. You can trust God to meet you in your hunger to know him in greater measure, just as he intended.

2
UNDERSTANDING GOD AS FATHER

This, then, is how you should pray: "Our
Father in heaven, hallowed be your name."
— Matthew 6:9

I have the profound privilege of being mother to four amazing children. Raising them and watching them grow is the greatest gift. Our youngest of two daughters is a beautiful, spunky warrior princess from China. I will forever have etched in my mind and on my heart the day we officially signed the papers so she could legally become a member of our family.

In November of 2012, we went to China to bring home our new daughter. Upstairs in a dusty government office, smack in the middle of China, we watched a surreal transaction unfold as we signed papers and converted American dollars to the Chinese yen.

As this process took place, our two oldest children played on the floor with their new baby sister, who had only been with us for less than twenty-four hours at that point. We felt like she was already one of our own. She was a tiny seventeen-month-old girl, and I watched with amusement as she crawled on the ground "playing tiger" with her big sister—both growling loudly as the official business of the adoption proceeded. The process concluded, and I gathered coats across the room. Then the orphanage director walked out of the office, turned around, and called my new daughter by her Chinese nickname, beckoning her to come say goodbye.

I can honestly tell you that time froze for me in that moment. I stood across the room from the director, bundling up my two older children in their coats, while our new daughter played at my husband's feet. There she was, my baby girl standing next to her brand-new daddy as the director called her by name. A fierce protection rose up in the pit of my stomach as I secretly, internally threatened this woman, *Do NOT call my daughter!* I had enough adoption education to know that this director, even though she likely meant well, was not helping the attachment process, nor was she diminishing the trauma and confusion of the moment by beckoning her to come hug her goodbye.

In those frozen moments, our sweet baby girl looked at her and looked at her new daddy. Then she wrapped her little arms tightly around her new daddy's leg, as if to say, *I choose him.*

If I could have yelled in joyful victory, I would have. Instead, I caught my husband's eye, and we invisibly high-fived across the room, rejoicing in her initial acceptance of us. She already knew—in less than twenty-four hours—that clinging to her new daddy, who was essentially a stranger to her, was already somehow better than anything she had ever known. This new daddy had just signed on the dotted line, paid the price to bring her home with us, and adopted her in every sense of the word—legally, emotionally, and spiritually. I would have *hated* to see what would have happened if that director had tried to approach her and remove her grasp from my husband's leg. Our heart to protect her and love her fiercely had already set in, and she was fully a part of our family.

SPIRITUAL ORPHANS

As followers of Jesus, many of us can relate to her experience of the hallmark day when we became a part of the family of God. Most of us can point to the day of our adoption into Christ, when we made the decision to receive Christ as Lord. That date might be written in our Bible; maybe we made the decision at church camp or walked the aisle one Sunday; or perhaps it was in college with the help of a mentor or in a Bible study during adulthood. Regardless of how it happened, we can point to our baptism, our signing a church membership book, or the invitation we felt when God beckoned our heart to him.

> How tragic, though, if all we ever know of our adoption is the date it happened.

If we only experienced a transaction with God when we officially became a Christian, we would have no relationship with him. Can you imagine the damage on my daughter's heart if she knew only of the day she was adopted and legally ours but nothing beyond that? Can you imagine our heartache if she knew only the initial attachment of grasping her new father's leg as she chose him—and that was it? If she had never heard his silly songs about her, or never knew the exhilaration of being whisked up on his shoulders so she could see the world? What would her life have been like if she never knew how he kissed her cheeks and how she would giggle uncontrollably as they played peek-a-boo? Or how he would sneak her candy, or how he told her she was beautiful? How he still does?

Adoption research says if we had never attached in close relationship to her or cultivated a connection with her, she would have lived in our home yet still would have felt orphaned. Yes, she would have legally been in our family, but she would have felt like an outsider. How tragic that would have been. How tragic it is for Christians who don't have a close relationship with God, just a date that secures eternity and a Christianity void of connection.

Perhaps this describes you. You recall the day of your salvation but struggle to connect with God. You know you should get close to him and secretly long for more but are unsure how to get there. Maybe you feel very far off from the promises of God, and his "good fatherhood" seems out of reach. You believe he is good in theory but think his goodness applies to everyone but you. But the good news is that when you realize how the messages of the world and your experiences impact your thoughts and feelings about God, you can allow God to define correctly how he wants relationship with you to look. And your capacity to know him can grow and build.

Those first few months home with our new daughter, I did everything possible to build our connection. She was traumatized and did not have a grid for what a mother and father should look like. We had to build it. I used finger puppets and songs, along with full-out Broadway musicals just to help her make eye contact and keep it. Connection was foreign to her, but I was determined to make it. And if I, being evil, know how to give good gifts to my child, *how much more* does our good Father God want his children to attach to him (Matt. 7:11)?

KNOWING GOD AS FATHER

Many of us have known good and bad parents, even if not our own. We've known good and bad churches, good and bad teachers, and good and bad mentors. Often, how our earthly parents raised us determines from a very young age our preconceptions of God as Father and how he feels about us. Sometimes, however, these notions simply do not line up with Scripture. God knew we would encounter roadblocks created by our earthly families that could derail a right and true relationship with him, so he gave us the capacity through prayer to continue to grow in our ability to attach to him, even into adulthood. Our heart can expand in love toward this good Father whom we long to know.

From the beginning, God's heart was about relationship. Of all of his glorious names, he prefers to be called "Father" in prayer. References to God as Father flood the Scriptures, and Jesus ultimately demonstrated this relationship in his instructions on prayer in Matthew 6:6–9: "But when you pray, go into your room, close the door and pray to your Father, who is unseen. Then your Father, who sees what is done in secret, will reward you." These are Jesus' absolute instructions on how to pray, and he chose to approach almighty God in prayer with *Father*. He bids us to do the same.

I'm sure that rattled the religious leaders of the day, who were fueled by a hierarchy of rules and regulations; hearing the ease with which Jesus spoke to the Father offended the structure they shakily stood upon. This relationship into which Jesus invites us and the truth of God's fatherhood should permeate our hearts and cause us to run to his open arms with a longing to be near to him. Only the Lord, our God, wants that intimate relationship with sons and daughters. He is Majestic Creator God, and he is at the same time, our most holy parent. In Exodus 4:22, we see this when God instructed Moses to tell Pharaoh, "This is what the Lord says: Israel is my firstborn son."

In Deuteronomy 1:29–31, God continued to define his identity as Father in this manner when Moses reminded the people:

> The Lord your God, who is going before you, will fight for you, as he did for you in Egypt, before your very eyes, and in the wilderness.

There you saw how the LORD your God carried you, as a father carries his son, all the way you went until you reached this place.

If we're honest, we often forget the provision of a perfect Father, like the Israelites did, and with grumbling forge our own way. We too are often rattled, like the religious leaders were, at the concept of nearness to God as Father in the secret places of prayer. Surely, we have to do something to earn that access. Can it really be that good? That true?

That the Most Holy God beckons us to call him Father and respond from that truth—we can barely wrap our minds around that reality of relationship and often struggle to get close to that level of intimacy with him. We were made to access the place in prayer where we don't just have knowledge of him as Father, but a knowing of him that comes from nearness. We know in our heads that the invitation of God as Father is true, but we wrestle to access that truth in our hearts. In theory we believe God is a good Father, at least in part, but our own life experiences haven't prepared us for that reality. We don't have a true standard of measurement for it, and we often fear the reality of his fatherhood exists for everyone but us. *He is Father*, we think, *but not for me.*

DISTORTIONS OF OUR HEAVENLY FATHER

Many Christians have an idea of God as Father that doesn't line up fully with God's full offer of that truth. There are distortions of God's identity as Father, some very damaging and some very subtle. For most of us, though, the root of our distortion of God's identity is a combination of attributing characteristics of our earthly fathers to our heavenly Father. We naturally assume they operate in the same way. These can be massive untruths that keep us distant from communion, or really small lies we believe because of how we were raised. It is part of our fallen human nature to do this.

Think of distortions like this: If you have one slow worker at the DMV, you assume they are all that way. This becomes your personal truth, whether or not it is really true. Yet I've had several DMV workers who were kind, efficient, and enormously helpful. Just because you experience one inefficient DMV employee, it doesn't mean they all are. But we are quick to project our experience with one on the group.

In a similar way, just because you experience distortions with the role of a father, it doesn't mean that God works in the same manner. In fact, he is so much better, so much more perfect in that role, than any mere human can be. He defined the role from the beginning. If we don't know him as the ultimate display of provision, protector, and provider from a place of close proximity, we will depend on our earthly representations of fatherhood to define the role. And even the best earthly fathers are flawed. So we are left with a lesser understanding of God the Father and walk away with false assumptions. We must let *him* define what his fatherhood looks like truly from the context of relationship. He has to become the grid by which we measure all other representations of "father," not the other way around.

We sometimes decide God must be like our earthly father because that is our natural paradigm. It's all we know, and it becomes our truth. Some of us have other earthly male influences—good, bad, and everything in between—and our experience with them becomes our standard measurement for how God responds to us as Father. For others, their church upbringing subtly (or not so subtly) influences how they think and feel about Father God for good or often not so good. We must take our preconceived notions before the true Father God and ask him to show us how those lies or misconceptions arrived there. Then we can ask for a true and right picture of who he really is as Father. This will help us to know him as he really is.

MEETING HIM IN THE INNER ROOM

Despite our insecurities and misconceptions, we can still hear the instructions from Jesus, "Pray to your Father" (Matt. 6:6). He adds in that same verse, "When you pray, go into your room, close the door." In the middle of this directive we see a sacred truth about the secret place of meeting God: when we pray to our Father, we go not only into our *physical* inner room and close the door to pray but also the *figurative* inner room of our hearts.

I'm a fan of interpreting the "go into your room" part of the verse both figuratively and literally. The people who matter most in my life get my time, intentionally and with my full presence. When we're together, I close out the world and steal away with them, and my attention is locked on that relationship. Sometimes, with the intimate relationships in my life, we will go someplace away from it all and leave behind every other distraction. I carve out time to build those relationships, without which I am incomplete.

This is true of my relationship with my husband, my children, my extended family members, and my close friends. Sometimes we retreat or go on vacation, but often, I spend intentional time during everyday life fixed on them without distraction. In these times, we put our phones away, turn off our computers, and sometimes even postpone our chores. I invest in these kinds of intentional moments because I love my people, and I know our relationships will not reach their full potential without these times of purposeful experience of one another. Those relationships will not thrive without time together.

In the same way, we as children of God must steal away to the inner room of our hearts to meet with our heavenly Father. Ideally, we can find a secluded place in our home for this, but even a bathroom or a closet will suffice! Once we cultivate relationship in that inner room of our hearts, we can return to it again and again. When we regularly practice this habit, the inner room of our hearts can flourish with the Father, even when we're outside of the literal secret meeting space.

RECEIVING HIS REWARD IN PRAYER

Jesus promised that when we pray, our "Father, who sees what is done in secret, will reward [us]" (Matt. 6:6). The progression goes like this: we go to our inner room to pray to our Father, and he sees us and rewards us. We have the security of knowing how God truly sees us in this place—something that we all long for. When our Father sees us, he responds by rewarding us.

> *God is not a passive participant in prayer.*

That reward of God is far better than we can imagine. The Greek word for "reward" in Matthew 6:6 carries several closely related meanings, such as "to compensate," "to reward for a loss or harm," "to give back," "to deliver," or "to return or restore."[1] All of the meanings of the word "reward" point to something far deeper than what we often get through a cursory reading. This word has a long-established precedent in Scripture and often relates to issues of justice.

The Old Testament understanding was that if harm was done to another person, the guilty party not only had to pay injury for injury but also ensure the wounded was healed and restored (Exod. 21:18–19). Psalm 18:20–21 shows the reward for keeping the ways of God with clean hands and not turning away from him. This idea of legal recompense can have a negative connotation, but remember, the Father we go to in prayer is the same one who "[prepares] a table . . . in the presence of [our] enemies" (Ps. 23:5). If we believe our reward for showing up to the secret place with God is based on our performance, then we miss it. Our posture with God in prayer should not be, "Look what I've done!" but, "Look at what I need."

Our acknowledgment that without him we desperately lack what we need prompts God to offer us a restorative reward that fills up empty places in our hearts, pays off a debt, and ultimately delivers what we lack. He lets us sit securely as he sets the table, prepares the food, and anoints our head. Our cup overflows as we receive abundance and nearness despite deserving eternal separation. We deserve recompense for every sin, but we're met by a good Father who has secured through Jesus that we owe nothing. We find restoration, reward, and repayment for loss because Jesus gave us access to draw near to the Father. This is truly good news!

Nestled right in the middle of the Sermon on the Mount, these instructions about prayer in Matthew 6:6 show us how God accomplishes what Jesus promised in the context of the sermon: he responds to our prayers to fill the one who is hungry or thirsty, bless the poor in spirit, and comfort the one who mourns (Matt. 5:3–6). When we come to him aware of our need, his response is to reward.

When was the last time you chose to steal away from the world and encounter your Father? When have you recently walked away from prayer with compensation for loss, deliverance, and restoration? Many of us don't come close to experiencing God in prayer like this. Yet this is our instruction for— and promise in—prayer. We can barely survive spiritually on quick utterances that we launch haphazardly to the heavens.

Contrast this with Jesus' teaching on prayer, which describes a relationship through which we receive what we need to fill a void. We should leave the prayer closet changed, restored, and seen by God. We should feel the grace of the reward that fills up the empty places and exchanges our losses for something we long for.

> What would it look like in our hearts, our families, our churches, and our cities if we walked in these truths?

If we walked as children of God, filled and not depleted? If we met consistently and intimately with our good Father? We would not only walk by the Spirit but also be an aroma to the world as connected sons and daughters of God (Gal. 5:25). We would get our very life from prayer with the Father in the inner room, and everything we do would be fueled by that life. The work of our hands, the words of our lips, and the very steps of our feet would be Spirit-filled and Spirit-led because we had encountered the Father. Success in all other spiritual disciplines and activities in the Christian life comes from this place of being known, seen, and restored by the Father.

PERSONAL PRAYER

1. Begin your time in prayer today by sharing with God your honest assessment of your attachment to him. Consider the adoption story in this chapter as your starting point. Do you find it difficult to wait on him? Do you struggle to make spiritual eye contact with him and stay connected to him throughout the day? Do you trust him? Do you want to be near, or are you more comfortable at a distance? Share your honest thoughts as it concerns connection to him. Don't filter them—he knows your heart even when you hide. Saying them honestly invites him into the conversation and opens the door for further growth in your relationship.

_____

_____

_____

_____

2. Consider your expectations as you approach God today in prayer. Do you expect the reward offered in Matthew 6:6, or do you somehow expect disapproval and rejection? Allow yourself to receive the truth that when you approach him in prayer, he repays, restores, and rewards you in your places of need. It is not his heart to respond otherwise. Once you've allowed yourself time to reflect on this truth, confess to him where you have struggled with the promise of his response and expected something different.

_____

_____

_____

_____

3. Reflect on your earthly father and other paternal role models you've had in your life, such as teachers, coaches, pastors, and supervisors. In what ways do they reflect a true example of the heart of Father God? Are there some characteristics that distort the image of God? Ask God to show you where your impression of him may have been skewed by these earthly relationships. Remember, it's not about blame or judgment but about recognizing that the reality of his perfect fatherhood can often be twisted by these very impactful earthly representations. Ask him for his clarity and insight so you may be able to see him rightly.

_____

_____

_____

_____

_____

_____

_____

COMMUNITY CONNECTION

1. Begin your group time today by allowing each member to share what benefits they have not accessed or sought after as an adopted son or daughter of God. For example, you might name some birthrights as an adopted child of God that you know are true but you have not accepted as your own, either because you feel they are out of reach or you aren't worthy of them. You could name things like, "I know God is good, but his goodness seems to elude me," or, "I know Scripture says I can get near to him, but that honestly sounds scary and overwhelming."

2. Share with the group one area of attachment to God in which you feel strong and secure, and one area in which you want to seek growth. For example, "I feel attached and secure in the area of trusting God, but I want to grow in my ability to just rest in his presence. I always feel I need to do something for him instead of just being still before him."

3. Take turns discussing specific areas where earthly fathers or father figures could have influenced your ideas about the fatherhood of God. These examples can be both positive and negative, such as, "Because my father picked me up every day after school and asked me a million questions about my day, I believe that God is interested in the small details of my life." Or it could be something like, "Because my dad was absent most nights of the week due to work, I believe God provides for my needs but isn't emotionally invested in my heart."

4. Be sure to conclude by praying for one another in the areas of need and where you feel a void in your identity as a son or daughter of God and in relationship with him as Father. Remember, God does not place a hunger for more of him if he doesn't intend to fill it. Pray from a place of confidence that you were made to walk as sons and daughters in right relationship with him.

You can stake a claim on knowing your truest identity as a child of God, who is the most perfect Father. Despite distortions that you've experienced, you can simply acknowledge them and attach yourself to the reality of God as Father. He knows the longing that you have for communion and he will be faithful to fill the void in your heart if you let him. He is good and his mercies endure forever.

3

EXPERIENCING GOD AS FATHER

I will be a Father to you, and you will be my
sons and daughters, says the Lord Almighty.
— 2 Corinthians 6:18

When my children were small and my husband had to go out of town for work or be absent for months at a time because he was in the military, he would take a small action figure with him and pose for pictures throughout his day with the figure placed in the shot. Sometimes its location was obvious and comical—perched next to a tourist attraction or peeking out of his shirt pocket in a meeting. But most often it was subtle and hidden, for the sheer joy of our children in finding it. They would wake up early anticipating a picture from their dad in my email inbox. It would often be the first thing they asked me about: "Did Dad send the picture?" They would laugh and crowd around to view it, seeking the hidden toy that was placed just for them to find.

Their father was physically distant but very present in this communication. They knew he loved them because he intentionally took something personal and displayed it, not only to make them laugh but also to remind them his thoughts were on his children and he was happy to do something that spoke to his personal relationship with them. His language in this game was their language, and it made the distance between them not so far after all. He knew they loved this simple act, and this act expressed his purposed communication and affection.

STARTING AFRESH

No matter where we are in our Christian journey, we long to communicate with our Father. As we wrap our minds around his roles as Creator, Provider, Ruler, and Holy One, we yearn for connection with him. To really know that despite his infinite omnipotence and dominion, he sees us and knows us as his beloved children. He knows us personally, and we know him. And we can grow in that knowing.

Regardless of where you start, you can connect with God afresh. No one ever arrives in their relationship with God. If anything, the more we encounter him in prayer, the more we recognize how vast his capacity is to meet us and how little we have experienced of it. We carry a longing only he can meet. Whether your concept of God as Father is true and secure or you have never entered into the inner room to meet him, you can still meet him right now.

Perhaps you have held him at a distance, unwilling to accept the reality of his fatherhood. You too can begin anew or build on what has already been established. A bad starting line simply does not exist with regard to prayer, and you cannot "do it wrong" or start from a place where the Lord cannot meet you. His heart beats for communion with you, and you must simply draw near to him, no matter how far away you feel or what weighs you down.

If Jesus instructed us all to pray in this manner in Matthew 6, the truth in his Word most certainly applies to us whether or not we believe it is true. His truth is solid and can be trusted. Remember, healthy human relationships do not remain stagnant or stuck; instead, they build and grow in intimacy. Our prayer life with the Father is the same: we were made to behold him and be transformed into his image from glory to glory (2 Cor. 3:18). To do that, we have to know him as he really is and authentically experience him in prayer. We cannot be transformed by God, be the aroma of Christ, or walk with the Spirit unless we encounter God in truth. We cannot become like him by simply thinking about him or reading about him; we were created *for communion with him*, so we must encounter him to be fulfilled and whole.

> *His heart beats for communion with you.*

> Communion means connecting with the Father.

We can attempt to be the aroma of Christ, but if we do so at a distance, our efforts will be found lacking and we will likely be half-hearted and exhausted in our striving. Our hearts will know it and be disappointed—we were not created to walk isolated and distanced. The lost world has a way of sniffing out counterfeit Christians quickly and can identify one who says all the right things but doesn't move in right relationship. We will fall short of moving in the fullness of our identity. It is communion with the Father that we must secure.

FINDING YOUR INNER ROOM

To pray in the manner Jesus describes in Matthew 6:6, I suggest finding a literal inner room. It doesn't have to be fancy, but learning to pray to the Father in this way requires intentionally pushing aside all other distractions. So find a favorite chair in the house or on the porch or a space in a closet or in a bedroom—anywhere that works well for you. To the best of your ability, determine that you will not be interrupted in this place.

We were created for communion with God.

Parents of young children, I can hear your laughter about this, which is why I included the phrase "to the best of your ability"! There is grace for your season, and it's okay if your children sometimes interrupt you. I believe one of the best discipleship examples my husband and I offer our children is being interrupted by them as they find us alone before the Father. Even if you don't have young kids, you may be interrupted by others when you pray, and that's okay too. Your room doesn't have to be a perfect fortress of solitude!

My literal place for prayer changes by season based on which window view I want or based on the school schedules of my children. Selecting a place based on these types of preferences is okay for you too. While you're in your place of prayer, also determine to close off the inner room of your heart by physically laying down distractions—your phone, other technology, and any thoughts or things that require something of you. Choose to close the door of your heart to everything else except the Father.

PRAYING "OUR FATHER"

Begin with a simple prayer by repeating Jesus' instructional words in Matthew 6:9: "Our Father." Let the reality of the Father in your life wash over you again and again. I recommend saying "our Father" repetitively until this biblical truth that he is your Father covers over all of your half-truths about him. The security of "our Father" washes away any place where you're worried that you're "not enough" or that he's somehow disappointed with you or that you somehow need to "do more" in order to please him. Allow the words "our Father" to permeate your distracted flesh and worried mind.

> Choose to align your will with his role as Father whether or not you feel like it.

When I do this, my heart eventually awakens to the reality of his fatherhood—as it reaches down through the layers of who I am into my truest self, which cries, "Abba, Father" (Rom. 8:15). You must allow yourself to go into these deep places through all of the distractions and protests that a stubborn soul might offer. By doing so, you are allowing the truth of God to dig deep through the noise into the place that was made to hold the experience of the Father—at the core of who you are. Your "inner man" longs for this reality of experiencing God, and you must mine the layers of your soul to get there and be renewed (2 Cor. 4:16).

Allow yourself time and practice to know God as Father in your heart. This is time well spent. It's completely normal if you have to deal with some pesky distractions and perceived inner resistance of the truth of his fatherhood. Keep repeating Jesus' words out loud—"our Father"—until they land deep in that place where you cry out for God your Father. You may want to adopt my personal practice, which is to say this phrase aloud until you sense the "peace of God, which surpasses all understanding" (Phil. 4:7, ESV). Here are three steps I've found helpful for experiencing God as Father in prayer.

1. Clear away distractions. If you experience distractions as you attempt to grow in your ability to pray and they sound loud in your mind, tame them in two very simple ways. First, shelve them during prayer. Use a simple prayer like, "I want to deal with this later, God, because right now, I am focused on knowing you as you really are. Can I place them on a shelf to take down and look at later with you?" Some distractions are valid concerns and items that need attention at a later time, and then some are just plain distracting. Communion is what we seek, and we must proactively clear our minds in order to focus on knowing the One with whom we seek communion.

Then, you can silence the protests of a stubborn will simply by declaring out loud something like, "I must meet with you, Father. I must get to you, my Father. You are all I want and need. My heart must be restored. I must behold you." These simple yet persistent declarative prayers can silence all other noise. There is life in them, and when you pray them, you are agreeing with who God is.

Like a young child who couldn't care less about what is happening in a room of adults when he interrupts his mother or father, we can have an incessant need to speak to our Father—and speak to him *now!* Our relentless declarations of simple childlike trust in God have a way of silencing distractions in us. The enemy seems to do anything and everything possible to prohibit this interaction between our Father God and us, his children. Do not be discouraged or dismayed by any emotional resistance or annoying distractions you might experience; instead, be encouraged that you are pressing into what you were made for—communion with a good Father.

2. Meditate on the Father's character. As you begin afresh in your prayer times with God, you can start by thinking about who God the Father is. You can do this by filling your mind with truths about him from Scripture. Perhaps you want to start by making a list of your favorite verses about God as Father to remind yourself of who he is. Some of my favorites are 1 John 3:1, Psalm 89:26, Matthew 7:9–11, 1 Peter 5:7, Isaiah 64:8, Ephesians 1:3—I could go on and on! As we take in these verses and remind our hearts of what is true about God, our expectation to meet him in the place of prayer rises.

You might also think about earthly examples of good fathers and their traits that fill your heart. I think of real-life examples of dedicated love like Dick Hoyt, the father who trained and competed in an Iron Man competition by the side of his quadriplegic son so he could conquer the race. That father bore the brunt of the physical work on his son's behalf. Then there was the dad who bought six different plane tickets on Christmas Eve and Christmas Day just so he could spend time with his flight attendant daughter who had to work over the holidays. That's not to mention the countless dads, like my own, who sacrificed time, sleep, and their personal pursuits to ensure the life of their children was better than their own. These examples show great love and sacrifice from fathers on behalf of their children.

As I reflect on that kind of love, I am reminded how much more our Father God loves us. I am moved by real-life stories, but the reality is, those examples pale in comparison to the love God has for us. The perfection of *his fatherhood* and the fullness with which he fathers us is overwhelming. It can be helpful to take good feelings and thoughts from earthly fathers and begin to attribute them to our heavenly Father, knowing they are but a glimpse of the all-encompassing fulfillment of his role.

3. Pay attention. As you think about the Father, pay attention to what comes to mind first. Often, your initial thought, unfiltered and unanalyzed, says a lot about what you really think about God as Father. You know cognitively what you are supposed to think according to Christian teaching, but the truth can still be a little distorted when you take an honest look. You know God is holy and good, but on a personal level, he can seem mad at you or distracted by more important things. You know these impressions are not true, but they feel true. Often those first impressions or initial thoughts get ignored or stuffed, but over time they can start to define who God is, whether you wanted them to or not.

How you feel *at first*, what you see *at first* in your mind's eye, what words *first* come into your thoughts—these initial inklings can be telling. They typically show us our real self. So take time with this step to gauge your initial responses to God as Father. He is a good God who doesn't manipulate. If your first thought or impression doesn't match Scripture, out of his great love for you he wants to show you the distortion. He will show you the root of why it's there and lead you to truth. There is no need to feel guilty if your truest response doesn't match who he is—you can receive the awareness as a grace from him and seek him for the truth. He wants to restore a true picture of his identity. If it doesn't "feel right" to think about him on the sensory level of what we see, hear, or sense, remember he designed our senses, in part, to help us encounter him.

God also created us with the ability to think about the ones we love naturally. When my husband was deployed in the Air Force, for example, my mind was filled with thoughts of him: what he was doing, where he was going that day, how he was feeling, and what his small bunkbed looked like. God created us to think about the ones we love, and to do so constantly. The part of us that does this so naturally was created to think ultimately about our Father God the most. We were made to do this. Allow yourself to do so and be honest with how you feel or what you see.

Again, there is no shame or condemnation if your picture of God doesn't match what is biblically true. A reason always exists for discrepancies between the truth in your mind and the truth of what you authentically feel. And at some point in time, someone or a life event distorted for you the truth of who God really is. The Lord's heart is to show you the reason for your false beliefs and restore them.

> *God created us to think about the ones we love, and to do so constantly.*

If this last step of paying attention to how you really feel is a struggle, don't worry. We *all* have roadblocks that are misaligned with Scripture, whether or not we know it. God wants to remove these thoughts and fill them with himself.

We will explore in latter chapters some valid reasons why the current discrepancies about Father God could be present in your mind. But for now, focus on what you know to be true. Focus on the truth of God's fatherhood in Scripture and even repeat "our Father" aloud as you begin renewing your mind in the Personal Prayer section. When you find yourself settling into this truth, let yourself just stay in that inner room and enjoy it. This is the place to become more like him and be transformed from glory to glory. It's where he restores you and forms you more into his image. Stay there, like a child curled up against a safe parent without the need to talk or ask questions, content just in being together.

PERSONAL PRAYER

1. Quiet your heart and ask the Lord to give you a sense of your starting point as you seek to draw near to him. As you set the eyes of your heart on the reality of your starting point, tell the Father your desire to move forward. You could pray something like, "Father God, when I stop and ask you where I'm starting from, I recognize that I know you're available but also that I stay at a distance. The distance between us isn't very far, but I realize it's still there. I don't want any distance between us. I want to draw nearer to you." Write down your starting point with the Father and your desire moving forward.

   _____

   _____

   _____

   _____

   _____

2. List some distractions below that seem to be persistent, and "shelve them." You can always conclude your time in prayer by talking to the Lord about them. Some distractions are just items you will accomplish later today. Placing them on paper gets them out of your head so you can fully focus on God.

   _____

   _____

   _____

3. As you quiet your heart and mind, begin to focus your attention on the Father. Try repeating the phrase "our Father" over and over again until the full truth of his identity goes from your head to your heart. What surfaced in your heart and mind as you repeated "our Father"? How did you feel doing this? Did you see, hear, or sense anything as you focused on the reality of his fatherhood in your life?

_____

_____

_____

4. What does your literal inner room look like? Where are you meeting with God today? Why did you select that place? Are there practical things that you could do to make it more appealing?

_____

_____

_____

5. Think about the Father and list a few of your favorite characteristics that describe him. List the items that come to mind that match his nature in Scripture, and feel free to add some of your favorite biblical descriptions as well.

_____

_____

_____

_____

6. Think about the Father, and list any thoughts that come to mind that you know do not match the truth of who he is in Scripture. They could be seemingly subtle misconceptions, but pay attention to those that feel slightly off. Over time they can create a large gap between you and God. List any of those thoughts below.

_____

_____

_____

_____

_____

7. Write a prayer of thanksgiving and declaration for where you've arrived today in your prayer life.

_____

_____

_____

_____

_____

COMMUNITY CONNECTION

1. Thinking back to when you first began to think about the Father in the Personal Prayer section of this chapter, discuss with your group: What images or feelings came to mind? Did you see in your mind's eye a storybook depiction of God? Did you sense him being distant or angry with you? Did you think about him as all-knowing but not personal? Did he seem uninterested or stagnant? Close and safe? Approachable? Take turns giving your first impressions of the Father.

2. If you found your thoughts about God as Father differed from Scripture, what might explain the discrepancies? Ask the Lord to show you the root of the false image of God by taking some time to quietly pray at the same time as a group, asking, "Where did I learn to believe that you were like that?" or, "Where did that come from?" Then share the responses with your group members. Remember most of us learned distortions of God by attributing characteristics of people in our lives to God, or learned them simply from the culture in which we were raised, both in and out of the church. As you feel comfortable, begin to share where these distortions about God as Father might be rooted.

3. If your image of God as Father feels distorted from what is biblically true, share with your group members the ungodly belief or lie behind it. Pause as a group and ask the Lord to help you name your major false belief about him. You might believe multiple lies, but which one affects you the most? It could be something like, "He's angry at me," or, "He is indifferent to me." Which has most shaped your relationship with him? Share your response with your group.

This week, practice going to the inner room with your Father who sees you and longs to restore you. Use what you've learned in this chapter to help you do this throughout the week. You can even use additional time to do this with your group today if time allows. Practice as a group and share what this looks like individually, cheering each other on before you continue individually throughout the week. You might have experienced a different impression today in your community than you did as you practiced alone when you drew near to the Father. That's okay and expected. God is vastly creative, and the depths of his heart to meet you are limitless.

Connection with God as Father is different for everyone, and there is no formula or "right way" to do it. Your way of knowing connection is that place deep in your heart that cries "Abba" and knows that he responds and meets you in those places of longing. That call and response of Father God to his child is personal and worth taking the time to pursue.

Remember that we are always growing in relationship with Father God. This growth takes practice and a continual stepping into the reality of his fatherhood. Don't be discouraged if your progress seems to move like small baby steps. Clearing out subtle misconceptions about him can be time-consuming, but it's worth it. We find freedom by knowing who God truly is and who we really are before him.

4

DRAWING NEAR

Draw near to God, and he will draw near to you.
— James 4:8, ESV

Years ago, we brought our newly adopted daughter home, as I mentioned. During that initial season of cocooning, we purposefully set out to connect as a family in whatever ways we could. One of our favorite ways to do this was to have a pizza and movie night on Fridays. We would spread out blankets and pillows on the living room rug and put pizza and cookies within arm's reach of everyone. It was glorious.

Given my neat and tidy personality, it was a big deal for me to make space for this sort of messy event. For those of you who are more laid back as parents than I am, this might actually sound like a normal thing. But with our four kids on the rug with melted chocolate chips and gooey pizza cheese all around, it was living dangerously for me! Pizza and movie night still remains the most requested activity in our family. With all of us snuggled up together, the rug is the best place to be.

Our newest daughter enjoyed it too but would persistently move herself right up to the edge of the rug—and no farther. She stayed on the floor, right next to the edge, without allowing even her toe to touch the rug. She was somewhat near to us as we snuggled in the middle of all of the food and fun, but not near enough. She would stay on the edge, watching and sometimes eating, but she would not get closer. If I tried to coax her or even place her closer to us, she would quickly make her way back to the edge.

Our sweet girl had totally valid reasons to stay at a distance due to trauma and transition, not to mention her having no grid for how a loving family does life together. Asking an orphan to suddenly trust the reality of a forever family is unrealistic, especially as abandonment was all she had known. As a result, she had built walls of protection long before I ever knew her.

I understood her pain as best I could, which broke my heart, so I resolved to make that time especially safe. I consistently encouraged her to come near us on the rug, but I wouldn't force her. We knew she was scared, but we took every opportunity to watch and welcome her. Then one Friday evening, without any special prompting, she willingly crawled up in my lap and stayed there. And I'm thankful to say that she has stayed near ever since.

OUR LONGING TO DRAW NEAR

We long to draw near to God, and we yearn to be in communion with him. Our first step toward this communion is to understand God as he really is—a loving and perfect Father, as I introduced last chapter, in all his majesty and authority. We must approach him with that understanding. The second step, which is equally important, is to actively draw near to him—the subject of this chapter. Communion with God is about intimacy and proximity, wholeheartedly knowing him in the fullness of who he is, and that we can only commune with him from a position of nearness to him.

> We were made to experience both.

Yet most of us limp through life with God and settle for scraps of the real thing because we do not know how to draw near to the Father. And even if we do know, we doubt deep down that we are good enough to be near him—or that he even wants to be close to us. But the Bible offers us wonderful truths to replace our false ideas about being near to God. Consider, for example, James 4:7–8: "Submit yourselves therefore to God. Resist the devil, and he will flee from you. Draw near to God, and he will draw near to you" (ESV). Let's look at the notion of proximity in James 4, where we find simple yet important steps toward ensuring our nearness to God.

> 1. *We must submit ourselves to God.* This means surrendering our own way to trust in God's authority. From my studies, I've seen how the original Greek defines the word for "submit" in two different

ways. In military procedures, it was used to define an arrangement of troops under a leader. In non-military contexts, it was also commonly understood as the voluntary attitude of giving in. Both types of definitions apply here as this verse has strong spiritual warfare significance (if we're near to God, the enemy flees) and also a personal acknowledgment of the connection between giving in to God to get near (our submission produces proximity). Submission opens the door to nearness when we understand we cannot fight in our own strength. This attitude of being both desperate and dependent is necessary for us to have a flourishing life of nearness to God.

2. *We must resist the devil.* When we submit to God, resisting the devil is much easier. Sometimes, it even becomes a non-issue. Our lack of submission, however, opens us to the enemy's schemes. By submitting ourselves to God, we acknowledge our complete dependence on him for protection, well-being, and peace. In our desperate submission to God, the enemy loses his hold. He thrives on our self-sufficiency and has little power when we voluntarily submit to God, who holds all authority over him. Submitting to God and resisting the devil are very effective in spiritual warfare, but our need for God's grace doesn't end there.

3. *God draws near to us.* The beautiful promise that follows is life-changing grace for all of us. When our posture is humble as we draw near to God, he willingly and quickly draws near to us as well. His heart seeks communion, and he does not delay, especially in our need. He doesn't require that we jump through hoops or prove our worth; instead, as our perfect Father, he meets us in our seeking.

This truth about God drawing near is often seen in Jesus' stories and teaching. The prodigal son, for example, came home to his good father, who waited and watched for him. Upon seeing his son, the father ran to him (Luke 15). Similarly, in Matthew, Jesus tells us, "If you, then, though you are evil, know how to give good gifts to your children, how much more will your Father in heaven give good gifts to those who ask him!" (Matt. 7:11). I know how to protect and defend my children, and most surely, I know how to receive them when they inch toward me from their need for assurance, identity, and love. I would never reject them in that place. How much more does God receive us and meet us when we draw near?

When our youngest daughter was seated on the floor at the edge of the rug, Friday night after Friday night, I was always right on the edge of the rug to receive her. I didn't make her crawl to meet me in the middle. But I desperately waited to hold her and bring her to where we were seated as a family. She didn't have to earn her place on the rug by crawling to the middle; she just had to decide voluntarily that being near to us was better. Then we lovingly welcomed her and stayed near to her in return. Our Father God works in the same way, only his response toward us is a powerful demonstration of the fullness of his love. This is a Father who says we can "come boldly to the throne of grace, that we may obtain mercy and find grace to help in time of need" (Heb. 4:16, NKJV).

> *The Father meets us in our seeking.*

God is our king, and history shows again and again that people didn't simply waltz up to a king's throne with audacious boldness. If anything, people waited for an invitation from the king and hoped the king was not in the kind of mood that would result in the loss of their life! Yet we see our perfect king and Father offer us an all-access pass to approach his throne without fear of punishment (1 Thess. 5:9). He offers the complete opposite response than the kings of this world! He offers nearness, not punishment. In the Scriptures I've mentioned here, and many others like them, we see the same tremendous invitation from God to come boldly to his throne and draw near to him without fear.

THE BELIEVER'S REST

When we recognize we can be near to God and that he responds by drawing near to us, a collective sigh of relief should come over us as children of God. We no longer need to struggle on our own and persevere isolated and afraid. We can truly rest in his presence and be filled. That rest is a product of being near and being known.

Hebrews 4:16 ends its chapter in the Bible with a helpful title often given by translators as "The Believer's Rest," which carries with it important implications and intricacies. This chapter describes a dichotomy between those who hear God's Word with faith and enter his rest, and those who do not enter at all. Some who "hear his voice" still harden their hearts in disobedience, unable to enter this rest on a specified day of judgment (Heb. 3:15). Still, "there remains a Sabbath rest for the people of God" that harkens to something encompassing *this* side of eternity (Heb. 4:9, ESV). "Let us therefore be diligent to enter that rest" (Heb. 4:11, NKJV).

Our present-day ability to rest, offered in this Hebrews chapter, is different than our eternal rest at the end of our life. As Christians we take great care to make sure we are going to heaven and can partake of that rest, while often missing the Sabbath rest available to us on this side of eternity. Hebrews 4 then reminds us that the Word of God is living, active, and sharp, with no creature exempt from the penetration of his Word (v. 12). The author says to consider Jesus, our Great High Priest, who understands our weakness and has passed through the heavens so we can approach the throne of grace to get mercy and help (vv. 14–16).

Thus, we are *to draw near to God*. This nearness to God, to receive mercy and grace in time of need, secures a lasting Sabbath rest on this side of eternity too. Yes, we have an eternal rest coming as sons and daughters of God, but there is much to embrace in this current Sabbath rest and in being near to God.

The order of events in Hebrews 4 reveals something profoundly good for us: a rest has been purchased, an eternal rest is coming, and we can access rest with him now. We tend to limit our understanding of that rest with him now to one day of the week—taking a Sabbath day of rest—when in reality, we can partake of that rest constantly through close proximity with the Father. We know this because verse sixteen would not make sense in eternity with God because we won't need to approach his throne needy and tired after we have stepped fully into his everlasting provision. We need that provision of mercy now.

Since we are to rest on this side of eternity, a Sabbath rest remains for us that is internal and abiding. This rest can only be found through Jesus, who made the way for us to draw near to the throne of God's grace. He allows us to have constant access confidently. This spiritual Sabbath rest is where we find abiding respite with God, despite our circumstances. Being able to approach his throne for help and mercy is vital, and he invites us to do so in close proximity to him with confidence.

Consider how we see this invitation to draw near also in Matthew 11:28, which says, "Come to me, all you who are weary and burdened, and I will give you rest." When we read this along with Hebrews 4, we learn that rest for a weary and tempted soul lies completely in drawing near to God.

> *We can partake of Sabbath rest constantly through close proximity with the Father.*

To finish the progression in Hebrews 4 of various ways that the believer rests here on earth and in eternity, the author ends with this final word in verse sixteen that appropriates this rest when we need grace and mercy. There is an eternal rest, there is a rest from labor on the Sabbath, but there is also an abiding Sabbath rest to be found in drawing near, which we are able to experience because of the finished work of Jesus, our Great High Priest.

BEING NEAR AND AT REST

If our youngest daughter had never made it past the edge of our rug, she would have never enjoyed our loving presence and provision for her. Instead, she would have grown up feeling second rate, or worse, like an orphan living in a home not feeling like she was fully part of the family. Most of us, sadly, find ourselves in the same situation—living outside of nearness to God.

What would it look like if my husband and I lived in the same house but never spoke to each other? Never looked at each other face-to-face? Never embraced each other or sat near one another? Close proximity matters in every meaningful relationship, and:

> The Father placed our longing for nearness in us from the beginning.

In Genesis, we find God walking in that garden tabernacle with Adam and Eve. Following their rebellion, God has ever since sought to fill our need to be near him by pursuing us. Despite our often unwillingness to be near, he still longs to gather us close. His heart is to dwell with us. He offers proximity, covering us with his pinions and providing refuge under his wings (Ps. 91:4). In the wilderness, God carried his children, "as a father carries his son" (Deut. 1:31), despite their consistent dismissal of him. No other god, no other king, no other master responds like that to wayward sons and daughters who repeatedly reject his offer of nearness.

SEWING NEARNESS

Years ago, I examined James 4:7–8 with my oldest daughter through prayer. As we read and prayed, the reality of this truth about God's nearness made sense to her by way of sewing.

The gift of sewing markedly skipped a generation from my mother and mother-in-law to my daughter. My daughter carries her grandmother's ability to see a pattern and stitch it beautifully. Me, not so much. When my oldest daughter sat before the Lord with these verses from James, she saw herself as a piece of cloth. She also saw another piece of cloth that belonged to God. She saw the Lord move her piece of cloth toward his, and then with a needle and thread sew them together.

My daughter shared this with me, and we talked about how the image she described held up under God's Word—that God really does the work. We voluntarily submit ourselves—so in a sense come near to him—but he does the real work of drawing our hearts close and joining us together with him. He created our cloth, and he is the most holy needle and thread.

Similar to how God's Word pierces our hearts and exposes our truest intentions (Heb. 4:12), the needle in her picture captures the truth that when we show up and willingly submit (James 4:7), God draws near and remains near to us. He knits us together through a covenant with us. Our response is small in comparison to his immediate protection, provision, and proximity.

Even the best earthly parents falter when their children reject their love. Our Father in heaven, though, "[makes] known to [us] the path of life" and "[fills us] with joy in [his] presence" (Ps. 16:11), and we come near to him, close enough to receive joy from his "right hand" (Ps. 16:11). And we have been brought near, and his presence is good and a refuge (Ps. 73:28). He always responds by drawing near to us when we draw near to him. He is "close to the brokenhearted" (Ps. 34:18), and our joy as believers—our good news—is that in Christ Jesus we "have been brought near by the blood of Christ" (Eph. 2:13). Not only do we obtain a reward when we get close to God the Father, but we also find rest despite our circumstances and the burdens we carry. He knows what we need and invites us to meet all our deepest needs in him. We must pursue the goal of drawing near.

PERSONAL PRAYER

This Personal Prayer section builds on what we practiced in the last chapter. As a reminder, go into the literal inner room you determined for this time with God in prayer. Also, prepare your figurative inner room so you're ready to meet with the Father. Close the doors of both rooms to ensure that your time with him is intentional.

As you did last time, start by thinking about the Father and all of his wonderful attributes. Remind yourself of what is true; if false thoughts arise, use your Scripture and characteristics list from last week to help you receive truth. Shelve distractions and misconceptions and continue to remind yourself of his goodness. Recite Jesus' words of prayer from Matthew 6, "our Father," until the reality of those words floods your mind, will, emotions—all the way to your core. Let his safety, peace, protection, and overwhelming love for you be your refuge.

1. As you think about the Father and his response to your drawing near, write down what you see, hear, or sense in your spirit as you approach him. Has it changed at all from the first time you tried this? What is your overriding emotion as you engage with God as Father? What do you see in your mind?

_____

_____

_____

_____

_____

_____

_____

2. Position your heart to draw near and dictate to your mind that your only purpose in these moments is to get close. Here you find rest and the deepest Sabbath. If you struggle with drawing near to the Father, stop and think more about Jesus. Why did he take up the cross? What was his end goal? Ask Jesus to help you receive what he has already purchased for you: access to the Father.

   Record your thoughts below as you do this. If you have conflicting emotions, give yourself permission to tell the Father out loud. Decide to be vulnerable enough with him to tell him things like, "I know this is true in theory, but I struggle to obtain it," or, "I've never thought about Jesus taking me near to you, Father God."

   _____

   _____

   _____

3. If your heart feels a bit divided at this point, it's okay and normal. There is always a reason for feeling that way, and while future chapters of this book should help you better understand the reason why, take some time now to ask God and see if you get clarity.

   I encourage all readers to continue posturing themselves in a place of voluntary submission before him. For many of us, this requires some discipline because we are so unaccustomed to truly submitting. If you feel blocked, try confessing to God any sin that feels present. He never demands that we try to clean ourselves up *in order* to meet with him; rather, his good pleasure is to wash us clean *as* we meet with him. If you feel blocked, ask him to show you why, knowing that in future chapters, we will explore in depth tools to help with the blocks that keep us from the Lord.

Ask the Father about a block that you feel and write any impressions or responses that you receive. If you don't perceive a block in your access to the Father, pause and wait on him and listen. Thank him for the close access to him through Jesus.

_____

_____

_____

_____

COMMUNITY CONNECTION

1. At this point of the study, what has been the most difficult step in connecting with God and drawing near? Do you know why? If relevant, try pausing as a group and asking why the particular step has been personally hard.

2. In the perfect Trinity, we receive grace, grow in grace, and have the capacity to absorb and keep grace. With which person of the triune God are you most at peace and feel the most comfortable? In the same manner, is there a person of the Trinity to whom it is difficult to draw near?

3. Similarly, with regard to grace, which of the following elements do you struggle with the most? Is it fully receiving the grace purchased for you by Jesus? Is it growing in grace through walking with the Spirit? Or is it keeping grace by continually renewing in prayer the truth of who the Father is? Identifying the nature of your struggle here will often reveal a deficit in some aspect of your relationship with the triune God, which will help you move toward restoration of that relationship.

Remember to rest in the truth that there is a simplicity in submitting to God and drawing near to him. His rest challenges our educated minds and religious pretenses. Many of us live in the United States, a culture in which people constantly compete for status and place. Many other societies of the world were also built on the worldly principles that motivate this type of competition, which stands far away from how the kingdom of God operates. It can take time and intentional practice in drawing near to God to undo the damage caused by years of living in this false system. To recognize that we bring nothing to the table and that he provides everything we need is humbling yet freeing. The Father's love is overwhelmingly good, and his heart to meet us is unlike anything we have ever known.

5

ABIDING AT THE TABLE

If anyone loves me, he will keep my word, and
my Father will love him, and we will come
to him and make our home with him.

— John 14:23, ESV

As I write this, it is December in Nashville, Tennessee. The temperatures outside are chilly, and we've already seen snow flurries in the air. My days and evenings are full of school performances and parties, and our family's schedule contains extracurricular practices and ministry opportunities in abundance. We're in the midst of the holidays, which brim with opportunities to have my heart both filled and depleted. I love the fullness of my days and all the people in my life. I am in a winter wonderland of activity and hustle and bustle, and even though all the activity causes me to fall asleep each day the moment my head finally hits the pillow, I dearly love it.

Home at Christmastime is the best kind of home. I am one of those who likes to have a Christmas tree visible from every room. So my own home has twinkling lights on our five trees throughout the house, with homemade ornaments that reflect our years as a family. We also decorate with wooden Advent pieces, stars, and candles. Then we enjoy hot chocolate and dinners at the table—where at least one tree is visible!

During the day when I'm out and about, I long to be home. I want to sit next to the warm fire in the fireplace and snuggle up with children while reading Christmas books. I often long for home throughout the year, but I fiercely protect the time there at home with my people as much as possible during the holidays. At the table, where my family lingers after eating, we talk about all sorts of things, from the comical to the most serious topics. We discuss everything from random tidbits of the day to what's going on in our hearts about what really matters in life. Everyone has a voice, and everyone gets a turn to be received and heard. It is the most precious part of my day.

My children love this time of the day too. I see the weight of their day come off their shoulders as we talk. I watch as they lay down any pretenses they might have carried through the door and simply be present. My husband takes off his tie and sits down, often for the first time that day, thirsty and hungry and ready to rest. I see my family in comfy clothes or pajamas, completely at peace and free from the expectations of their day. I still myself and feel joy coming back in the places of my heart where the day might have attempted to take my joy away. Our family is connected, at peace, and happy just to be in one another's presence.

As good as our home is, it is just a taste—*just a small glimmer of the reality*—of what God offers to us as we abide with him.

AT THE TABLE OF GOD

I love the word "abide." I have sat with that word for years now, and there is always more to gain from the mystery and gift of abiding with the Lord. I still feel that I have just scratched the surface of the treasure of embracing the riches of this reality of being at home with the Father, Son, and Holy Spirit. From the beginning of time, God's heart has always desired to dwell with his children. The magnitude of an almighty God who wants communion with us should cause us to worship. That he would even want to be with us is a beautiful gift, let alone that he actually seeks abiding with us in nearness and intimacy.

As I mentioned previously, in Genesis, God walked in the garden in the cool of the day with Adam and Eve, who were surrounded by his perfect love. In the Old Testament, God declared his intent to dwell with the people of Israel and not forsake them (1 Kings 6:13). The psalmist understood the blessing on one whom God chooses to dwell in his courts (Ps. 65:4). In Revelation, the city of God is among men, and God dwells among them (Rev. 21:3). And in one of my favorite passages, the Lord declares, "Behold, I stand at the door and knock; if anyone hears My voice and opens the door, I will come in to him and will dine with him, and he with Me" (Rev. 3:20, NASB).

ABIDING AT THE TABLE

The common yet lavish grace of God is available to all of us. God has always loved us—from the beginning of time to everlasting. He wants to dwell with us and extends an ever-present invitation for us to abide with him.

When Jesus promised to make a home with us in John 14:23, mentioned at the beginning of this chapter, we received the promise of the Trinity making a continual stay with us. Pause and consider the magnitude of the gift of the Father, Son, and Holy Spirit choosing to remain at the table with us in friendship and fellowship. This is our birthright as followers of Jesus and one that we do not access often enough.

> *The common yet lavish grace of God is available to all of us.*

We may visit that dwelling place from time to time, especially in a crisis, but we struggle *to remain there.* Remaining in a place of abiding is where we were meant to find life-giving connection and be filled from the source of all grace and power from the Trinity. If we believe Jesus when he said, "Apart from me you can do nothing" (John 15:5), we will never stray from the Vine. Growing in relationship and understanding the tremendous gift of abiding is essential to our fruitfulness. Our dependence on remaining determines our connection and, consequently, our joy as sons and daughters.

> Abiding is the antidote to the unsatisfied Christian life.

Every other "god" demands that we bring something to the table, that we have to earn our place while they remain out of reach. *Our* God, however, chooses to live with us. He always has. Think about what it means to dwell together at a table. At my own dinner table, there is laughter, crying, and everything in between! We have deep conversations and listen to mundane recountings of the day. We share feelings and hopes; we experiment with thoughts and opinions and form them too. And there is often a comfortable silence, an ease in just being in the company of the ones I love. How much more are we able to settle, rest, and be sheltered under the Father, Son, and Holy Spirit.

When we love Jesus and obey him, then he and the Father will come "to make [their] home" with us. The Greek word for "make" here translates to "be the author of, to make ready, to prepare and shoot forth, to ordain and appoint."[2] By definition, there seems to be an important transaction that occurs when we abide with our Lord: a holy preparation in which God writes on our heart, makes us ready, and from his table shoots us forth into the world both appointed and ordained. We come empty and dependent, and he sends us out to do what we cannot accomplish ourselves.

Sadly, however, most of us try to author our lives with a narrative that moves away from his table. We manipulate our God-written story and decide to do things on our own. At best we hope for a little anointing, try to get by with some fast and easy fruit of the Spirit, or take a quick drive-by with the Lord to get him to sign off on our plans—but only to appease our conscience. God's table is not designed for quick visits but for long stays; we were made to linger. He calls us to live there continually. It is the place we long for, protect, and where we dwell with him. This internal place of rest and communion should go with us and permeate all other places and destinations. It is where our hearts overflow, and where we are deeply known. From this home and dwelling with the Lord all fruit comes.

Yet so often we busy ourselves with religious activity and wonder why our relationship with God is not flourishing. We wonder why it feels dismal and draining. But only at the table of the Lord are we truly connected to the Vine— apart from whom we are actually doing nothing, even if our calendar is filled with a lot of somethings (John 15:5). There is kingdom work to be done—but it must be done from this place of rest and abiding if we are to work differently than the world does, full of the fruit of the Spirit.

> *God's table is not designed for quick visits but for long stays; we were made to linger.*

The Lord says his presence will go with us. He tells us spiritually through Christ what he told Moses, "I will give you rest" (Exod. 33:14). From his table, which is both internal and spiritual, we find our solution to disconnected and disappointing striving. At his table the fruit of the Spirit is prepared and offered; we must linger there with him so he can do the work we cannot. As Hudson Taylor so aptly stated, "Let us never forget that what we are is more important than what we do."[3] We know who we are and whose we are by abiding at the table of God.

ABIDING AT THE TABLE

PERSONAL PRAYER

1. The reality that the Lord condescends to our level by choosing to make his home with us should cause us both to worship him and be overwhelmed by his love. Even with the offer of being at home with God, many of us stay far from the table—and far from him.

   Metaphorically, do you stay just outside God's home by the smelly trash cans, always looking in the window, believing that this home exists but just not for you? Is the house visible but far from you as you are stuck in rebellion or cynical spiritual homelessness? Are you in the wretched middle of indifferent Christianity? Do you remain with one foot in the front door and one out in the cold?

   In order to abide for the first time or to increase your capacity to abide, ask the Lord, "Please, show me where I really live most of the time." This is a place where you have grown comfortable living away from him. Record what you see below.

   _____

   _____

   _____

   _____

   _____

   _____

2. Once you have a sense of where you typically make your home, ask yourself if it aligns with the Lord's desire to dwell with you. If it doesn't, then confess that to him now. Ask him to grow in your heart a longing for abiding with him. And ask God to give you a sense of what his love really looks like in that place of abiding. Write out your desire to dwell with God and your heart to be at home with him. It could be a simple prayer like, "God, I stay on the outskirts, but I want to learn to be myself at the table with you. I have a seat there and want to learn to remain."

---

3. Finally, position your heart to abide with God. God gives you physical senses so you can understand, even if in a small measure, what it feels like to be safe and secure and at home with him. In this chapter, I described my home at Christmas, how it looks and smells and how I feel there. Take those physical responses as a model, then pray your own prayer of longing to the Lord. For example, you could pray:

> *Lord, I know what home feels like on earth. And that is sometimes great and sometimes hard. But I know that even the best of days at home pales in comparison to abiding with you. I submit to your home because I know that I long for it and that I was made to dwell there with you. I don't know what it looks like, but I know that I want to be there consistently. Will you abide with me and show me how to be at the table with you? I want to live there; I must live there. This is the cry of my heart.*

As you wait and listen for the Lord, record any thoughts or impressions about God's offer to abide with you. Begin writing what this home with the Lord looks and feels like.

_____

_____

_____

_____

_____

COMMUNITY CONNECTION

1. Do your earthly home and table provide a positive or negative jumping-off point for thinking about abiding with God? Why?

2. If you weren't used to being at home with God prior to this study, how did it look and feel to try abiding with God during the Personal Prayer exercises? If abiding with the Lord was familiar to you, did you find greater depth in your ability to remain with him? Did images come to your mind? What was your overriding emotion?

3. Once you landed in that abiding place with God, were you uncomfortable or tempted to leave too soon? Why?

4. Discuss the truth of John 15:5 and your personal reality in remaining attached to the Vine. Do you find that you exist there or come and go? Can you determine the reason why remaining with him is difficult?

> Every step closer to abiding is a good step. If you struggled to get to a secure place with the Lord, continue to ask him for that security, and if you're not living with him, ask him to show you why you live in the distance away from the table. He would not place in you the desire to abide with him if he didn't intend to fulfill it. You can trust his timing and purposes. There is no failure in "not arriving." May we never "arrive" in abiding! Consider it a success simply to acknowledge that there has been a distance between you and God and that you now want the real thing.

PART 2

THE CORE

The most magnificent physical landscapes don't become beautiful overnight. Intentional maintenance produces its growth and beauty. The landscape of our heart was made for abundant life. Thus, we need to actively allow God to remove anything that would threaten the landscape and cause death and decay. In this part, pursue freedom in the main areas of your life where you experience strongholds due to wounding, entanglement, sin, and ungodly beliefs. These pieces are Core tools in Freedom Prayer ministry, which has always been life changing to me. Learning to use these tools is essential to cultivating a wholehearted prayer life.

Learn more about Freedom Prayer's ministry at freedomprayer.org.

6

WOUNDING: THE TRASH

Above all else, guard your heart, for
everything you do flows from it.
— Proverbs 4:23

Our house sits off of a major road in the city of Nashville. Backed up to that road is a field of beautiful green grass, separated by a creek and tree line. We knew when we bought the house that the Lord was leading us to this sanctuary and that it would be a place of rest, not just for us but also for many who would come through our door. I love looking from my bedroom window at the field, which is on the other side of the creek and through the trees. Lines of mowed grass look like a basketweave of verdant beauty.

The serenity I find in my surroundings gets abruptly jarred when—more often than I'd like to admit—someone driving by decides to toss their trash on our field or, even worse, *right on our front yard*. When this happens, the injustice of it stares at me from every window of my home; I couldn't ignore it if I wanted to.

Trash thrown right on the front lawn! It seems ridiculous. While I could easily give a speech entitled "What Has Become of the Human Race?" prompted by this issue alone, trash on the lawn is just a symptom of a bigger issue. The bigger issue we wrestle with is the injustice of having to deal with someone else's trash. This may not be very Christlike of me, but I have plotted—along with our two boys—to place a hidden camera in the trees by the field to catch the trash-throwing fiends in action. We also thought of placing a large sign in the field that says "Jesus Is Watching You" and seeing if that makes any difference.

On more than one occasion, my boys have walked the perimeter of our property, looking as forlorn as possible, picking up everything from beer cans, soda bottles, water bottles, and even a pair of men's underwear one time! (Please do not get me started on that.) Often, my boys pick up the trash in their church clothes for added effect, in hopes of making the culprits feel really guilty about their littering if they happen to drive by.

When we arrive home and find trash on our property, we all feel disappointed and angry. It simply does not seem fair that we have to deal with the consequences of someone else's poor choices. It feels unjust. All of this becomes an obstacle to our peace. We must deal with these injustices that take our time and energy. We see the trash on the lawn, which is inconvenient, but we are most afflicted by the fact that we must now respond and take action.

GOD'S RESPONSE TO THE TRASH

In the grand scheme of things, trash on the lawn is no big deal. But consider what emotional "trash" can do in our lives. We find pieces of trash like this in the places where someone has mindlessly or deliberately wounded us. Perhaps they acted as if their actions carried no consequences in our lives. We have all been wounded at some time or another. For some of us, the actions that caused our wounds were relatively minor but still made a lasting impact on us. For others, the wounds were deep from the beginning, with longstanding, repetitive, and traumatic, life-long consequences.

Many people have been on the receiving end of cruelty, rejection, slander, abuse, abandonment, and general meanness. They are left to deal with the effects. Injustice can rise up within us like a fire. That fire can be much worse when we not only have to deal with hurt we didn't ask for but also the knowledge that the person who wounded us seems to live their life as if nothing happened. Sometimes we deal with those consequences for days or weeks; quite often we deal with them for years. It feels wrong in every way.

It *is* wrong. And we love a good God who sees the wrong and responds. Our God is "close to the brokenhearted and saves those who are crushed in spirit" (Ps. 34:18).

Consider the truth that he is near and responds to those who are crushed by their woundedness. Another psalm shows that God "heals the brokenhearted and binds up their wounds" (Ps. 147:3, ESV). In whatever way we might have been wounded, God responds the same way:

> He draws close and brings healing.

OUR RESPONSE TO THE TRASH

So what should our response be to God when it comes to our places of wounding? Reflect on what would happen to my lawn and field if we didn't pick up the trash. What if we decided that because it was unfair, we simply would not respond to the garbage on our property? *I didn't throw it there, so it's not my responsibility to pick it up.*

When my husband and I signed the deed to our property, there was such peace and joy. It now belonged *to us*. It was now *our property*. Technically, our names are on the title, and we own the land. Because it is ours, we are responsible to tend it, no matter what happens. We do this in order to maintain the serenity of the land that drew us to it the first time we saw it. If we didn't tend to it, eventually a few pieces of unsightly trash would multiply and garbage would take over. When we bought the land, it became ours to take care of and watch over, to guard and preserve.

In the same manner, when someone wounds us, we have to respond to what was thrown on our heart. We have been "bought at a price" (1 Cor. 6:20). The property of our heart belongs to Jesus, who graciously equips us to guard it and tend it. Even if my physical lawn was covered in garbage, underneath it all, I still own it and the rights to it. And just as nothing can separate us from Christ's love (Rom. 8:39), the unsightly trash in our hearts due to wounding cannot separate us from God. It threatens to at times, but God owns the property of our hearts and partners with us to tend it. No matter how bad our wounding, how traumatic our experience, or how painful our relationship with someone, our identity is secure with God.

The issue of the trash remains, though. It has to be picked up and disposed of. In our anger or pain—right in the middle of the feelings of injustice—we typically do not handle cleanup very well on our own. While I might walk

> *The property of our heart belongs to Jesus.*

through my muddy field to grab a huge Styrofoam cup nestled on my property line, I'm not really interested in recycling it or making sure it goes where it should. This is because I'm mad, and my perspective has become clouded. I need to not see it anymore and don't really care about where it should go. In the same way, in order to find healing, we have to give God permission to see our wounding, name it, and take it out of our hands because our perspective is distorted. There is a process for waste management, and it is important. Sorting through the trash in our heart is practical and freeing.

SORTING THROUGH THE TRASH

The process of sorting through the trash of our hearts falls into three steps.

1. Acknowledge it. In order to deal rightly with trash, we have to acknowledge its reality. Sometimes in our efforts to move on, we deny the existence of our pain, even though we encounter it daily. Sometimes we do this from a place of self-protection, believing that if we were to acknowledge it, it may get worse—or become too much to bear. At other times, we respond to our wounding from the belief that we should "get over it" and move on.

If we were raised in a family that operated from a creed of "buck up and stop your crying," it can be difficult to allow for the simple acknowledgement of our pain. Likewise, if our belief about God is that we cannot go to him with our struggle or wounding, we will deal with it in isolation. Our only recourse is to "stuff it," even though most of our woundings are too loud to ignore. They demand to be acknowledged one way or another. We are left helpless, and as a result, we often feel guilty that we cannot move on.

2. Name it. When we finally are able to acknowledge our wounding, naming the offenses can be difficult. We can fall into one of two traps here. We either downplay the intensity of the pain, or we embellish the wounding and make it more than what it is. We do this from a place of a deeper, unresolved need that the current wounding hits like a bruise. We are often unaware that we are reacting from those old wounds. On the other hand, when we downplay the magnitude of what happened, we normally do this from a place of comparison, such as thinking, *Mine was bad, but other people have it way worse.* Sometimes, we don't properly name the wounding because we haven't found a safe place in which to name it; in other words, denying the gravity of hurt feels safer.

For example, I have prayed with far too many victims of abuse and trafficking who have been unable to rightly name the wounding because their innocence was stolen at a young age, and they accepted this harrowing reality as normal behavior. As children they had not yet developed a grid for what healthy relationship looked like, so their reality was all that they knew. They never found a safe place to name the injustices inflicted on them because so many people had called it "normal." Their abuse is far from normal, and in order for their healing to occur, they need a safe place to call it what it is.

Whether our wounds are large or small, we all need help in naming them, and God is ready and willing to give gentle wisdom in those hurts that we struggle to name. He sees all, knows all, and is not blinded by false labels or twisted realities that we've held.

I've prayed with many people who've found that God's ability to name the wounding was exactly right and much better than our ability to do so. For example, I may be angry because a close friend continues to belittle the work I'm doing. I may call it "rude," but when I ask the Lord why it hurts, he can show me that it hits a long-standing wound that has been around since childhood of being unseen and made to feel small. He has the ability not only to name it correctly but at a deeper level than my cursory explanation about rudeness being painful; he brings the true restoration that I may have been blinded to in my quick assessment in denial of the pain; and he provides exactly what I need.

Similarly, when we struggle to name our pain correctly because we are embellishing it, God can name it correctly and point to the root cause of why we feel the need to embellish. For example, consider the countless people who are overlooked for a promotion or a new position and how that wounding can fester and become more painful than it should be. It hurts for sure, but it can often hurt much more if it's hitting an old wound of rejection that has been repeated over and over again in the person's life.

Again, God's ability to point to the source of our pain and name it is truly unmatched. He can set the wounding right by clearly naming it for us, which enables us to name it too. Naming the wounding doesn't make it worse; instead, it places the wound of our heart in the hands of a gracious God, who is equipped to help us deal with it properly. We are not alone in this process, but we have to submit to God's offer of help.

3. Dispose of it. Once you've allowed God to name the wounding, we must not continue to hold onto it. The pain only festers and rots in our hands. Placing it in his hands doesn't *dismiss* the wrong but allows God to hold it. He is perfect in his balance of justice and mercy, and able to bear the weight of the wound and carry what we simply cannot. The wound is safer in his hands, and he knows how to dispose of it properly.

YIELDING TO THE MASTER GARDENER

Think of the various ways you throw out everyday trash, recyclable items, compost at home, or how you might even haul away large pieces of junk. When we allow God to hold our woundings, he can decide where they go and how to remove them completely. Often this is best done in community, with a few friends praying together for properly naming the wounds and how to dispose of them. Many of the issues that we encounter in Freedom Prayer are wound based; it is not accidental that the enemy works over a lifetime to inflict pain and destruction. Some of us have extremely traumatic woundings that require a layered and stepwise system to break them down properly. That system could involve a variety of methods to heal—such as a combination of what we do through Freedom Prayer ministry, therapy, recovery groups, and ongoing community. This is not the everyday trash on our lawn. These pieces require a certain kind of care.

As I write this, I recall many adults with whom I have had the privilege of praying and watching God unlayer the years of wounding caused by a parent who verbally abused them, left them as a child, or violated them. I can recall countless marriages that were abruptly shaken by hidden sin, affairs, addictions, and secrets. God's ability to name and hold the depth of their loss is one of the reasons why I love him so much—this ability to hold what we cannot and his heart to do so willingly. This makes him unlike any other "god."

> Our words fail to describe that kind of holy compassion.

Some of us have an "everyday" sort of wounding that wasn't so bad in reality, but it has sat on the landscape of our heart for so long that now it has produced damaging consequences. Consider the person who was told something demeaning by an admired teacher, or a friendship that was damaged over misperceptions and was never the same, or a seemingly happy marriage that was distant and cold. Those wounds aren't necessarily traumatic, but they can carry long-term damage when not dealt with. Again, in my experience, God is so gentle as he takes these wounds and disposes of them rightly. He is available to us through prayer. We need this nurturing of God to help us with our wounding, no matter how big or how small we might perceive it to be.

We naturally dispose of trash, regardless of how it got there in the first place, but with our wounds, as much as we say we want to get rid of them, we often can't let them go. We feel a false sense of vindication by holding on to that sort of trash because somewhere deep down we know it doesn't belong. We believe that by holding on to the pain we are getting revenge on those who wronged us.

As I imagine the spoiled and entitled teenager who flippantly tossed their Styrofoam cup filled with iced tea on my lawn (I'm just guessing here), it seems fair to continue to be mad and hold him responsible. Because if I don't, who will? The truth is that littering teenagers, like the people who have wronged us, usually don't give their actions—or us—a second thought. They've moved on long ago. Yet our hearts want justice, and the false sense of atonement we feel when we keep the memory of their trash front and center doesn't usher in God's healing.

In actuality, our hearts get covered like a landfill day after day. Trash begins to fester fast. The active process of allowing God access to the places in our hearts that are wounded is the first step to freedom from that pain. God never intended for us to tend our hearts alone. He is a Master Gardener with a proven system of waste management. But we must let him in. When we do this, he can acknowledge it, name it, and dispose of it—and everything that came with it. In the next chapter, I outline the full steps for disposing of the trash, but for now, let's begin the process of disposal by simply acknowledging that the trash is there and that we need God's help to remove it.

God is available to us through prayer.

PERSONAL PRAYER

1. Begin this personal prayer session by taking a survey of the land of your heart. God has created it and given you the responsibility of guarding it well, "for from it flows the springs of life" (Prov. 4:23, ESV).

   In a figurative sense, walk around your property and ask the Lord to name any wounding that is blocking your life with him—any place of pain or where someone has hurt you. For example, you can write down people or events as they come to mind and list them chronologically around the drawing below. There aren't specific rules to this exercise. You can simply list wounds as they come to your mind and as the Lord reveals where trash might have been thrown on your lawn. Here are some categories you can use for them.

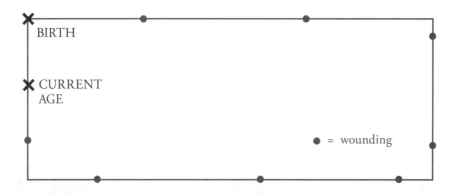

WOUNDING	PERSON RESPONSIBLE

2. Pay attention to your overriding emotion with each place of wounding. Is it anger? Hatred? Sadness? Grief? Disappointment? It may be helpful to attach the emotion to the event as well. Ask the Lord to help you name the overriding emotional response to each significant wounding and write it next to the corresponding event.

WOUNDING	PERSON RESPONSIBLE	EMOTION

3. Jesus gives us a glimpse of his heart for the wounded in Luke 15 as he describes the lost coin. When we are wounded, like a lost coin, we are forgotten and discarded, consumed by the darkness, isolation, and dirt we find ourselves in. But we were never meant to be lost. Jesus' response to that neglect of being tossed aside is relational and freeing. He illuminates the darkness and reminds us of our value, despite our wounding or pain.

Read the lost coin parable in Luke 15:8–10. Then ask the Lord what you have falsely believed about yourself because of your woundings, especially the major ones or the ones that have been present for a long time. Ask him to help you name those false and ungodly beliefs that remain with you on the landscape of your heart.

WOUNDING	PERSON RESPONSIBLE	EMOTION	LIE

COMMUNITY CONNECTION

1. One of the most vulnerable moments in community comes when we expose to one another our pain and wounding. Fear due to possible rejection or embarrassment can be overwhelming. Yet I've repeatedly seen the Lord almost instantly unite a group in support of one another. That first step of sharing is often very healing on its own. While it can be difficult, tell your group what you *fear most* about sharing those wounded places. Some possible fears are, "I will be misunderstood," or, "I will be embarrassed and alone," or, "My wounding is really traumatic and I'm not sure if I'm safe to share it."

2. Do your best to share the landscape of your heart with your group members. It could be one place or multiple areas the Lord named during your personal prayer, where you were the recipient of unwanted trash being thrown at you. As you listen to others share, remember to listen quietly and without judgment. Listen with intentionality and honor—it is a privilege when others share their most painful places. Listen well and share bravely.

3. As your leader directs, stop and pray for any individual who would like prayer. There are no rules here; just pray for encouragement, protection, and exhortation that the Lord will indeed finish what he starts while tending to their pain.

   Declare the truth that God is faithful to reveal our woundings and give help and hope. He is indeed near to the brokenhearted and quick to bind up our wounds. Your freedom from pain, bitterness, and heartbreak are God's to freely give. The author and perfector of your faith will not write your story and leave it unfinished. In his hands, he can complete his work of restoration. If you submit your heart to him, he is faithful to fill it anew.

7

FORGIVENESS: THE RESOLUTION

This is how my heavenly Father will treat each of you
unless you forgive your brother or sister from your heart.
— Matthew 18:35

As much as we don't want it to be true, sometimes forgiveness really is a heart issue. We can say the "right" words all day long, but if we don't actually forgive at the heart level, our actions will not follow our words. We will still act on what we feel, which is hurt, unless we forgive from the heart. Our hearts drive us in what we really believe.

From a young age, for many of us, we learn that Jesus forgave us, and we accept that we should forgive others too. His forgiveness motivates our forgiveness of others, and that cause and goal—forgiveness—can be ingrained in us from childhood. Yet we might still struggle with this. Forgiveness is just not that easy. Most children are instructed in sibling squabbles to say, "I'm sorry." And then following the initial apology, the sibling who was wronged, or maybe just didn't get caught, is told to say, "I forgive you." In a perfect world, that is that and everyone moves on.

In reality, though, kids don't move on, and we as adults don't either. We mature and sit in a church service listening to Scripture's instructions to forgive "seventy-seven times" (Matt. 18:22). In conviction, we internally say we forgive the person who caused us pain. That person is sometimes sitting in the same row with us. We say it because we know we are supposed to and because we know there are consequences if we don't. We say it, but we still feel wretched because even though we said it, our heart still carries the weight of the wrong. We walk away feeling guilty and disillusioned because just saying, "I forgive you," didn't really give us the relief we had hoped for.

> Our heart has to buy into the idea
> of forgiveness to get freedom.

For the heart to truly forgive, we have to see forgiveness as Jesus saw it. He offers the ultimate example of forgiveness in the cross, which solidified his authority on the issue. No other person has ever—or will ever—forgive to the level that Jesus did. We must allow him to disciple our hearts into true forgiveness. This is Jesus who "canceled the certificate of debt consisting of decrees against us, which was hostile to us; and He has taken it out of the way, having nailed it to the cross" (Col. 2:14, NASB).

Something about the way Jesus forgives is much more active than the quick verbal response that we have been trained to mutter. The passages about his forgiveness contain a series of verbs: he "*canceled* the certificate of debt," he has "*taken it out* of the way," and he "*nailed it* to the cross." His all-encompassing, active forgiveness does not just pay lip service to us; no, he gets personally involved in forgiving us.

We see this pattern of actively dealing with the debt and removing it also in the parable of the unmerciful servant in Matthew 18:21–35. The catalyst

We must allow Jesus to disciple our hearts into true forgiveness.

for this parable comes from Peter's question to Jesus, "How many times shall I forgive my brother or sister who sins against me?" (v. 21). Like all of us, Peter was looking for a number so he could check it off his list and perform his due diligence of moral requirements. So Jesus told the parable of the servant who owed a great sum of money and the king's response to him as he settled his accounts. The servant who owed the king much was unable to pay his debt, so the king ordered that the servant and his family *be sold* in order to repay it. The servant, on his knees and distraught, begged the king to be patient and allow him time to pay it all back. The king felt compassion, released him, and canceled the debt.

This parable gives us marching orders for true forgiveness, through an active and layered approach, so we can wholeheartedly pardon the one who wronged us. Unfortunately, this servant in the parable turned around and held another servant responsible for a debt owed to him and demanded that he pay back the small amount he owed. Right after the king had pardoned him completely, he threatened harm to another. And while we like to judge this wicked servant, we would all be wise to place ourselves directly in his shoes. The wicked servant who had been forgiven much refused to exonerate his fellow servant over something small. If we're honest, we've all been there.

> Like the wicked servant, we've all failed to offer the forgiveness we've fully received.

And here's the interesting reality in this story about debts and their being canceled (or *not* canceled): someone is always watching. Other servants watched the wicked servant choke the man and throw him into prison. In their grief and disbelief, they reported back to the king what the wicked servant did. Likewise, when Jesus, in Colossians 2:14, canceled our certificate of debt, we also know that powers and authorities of all kinds, especially in the unseen world, were watching. And as Jesus deliberately walked out the steps to cancel a hostile debt against us, those powers who had their gaze fixed on his every move were mocked. In fact, they were publicly humiliated. You can cheer here—this is really good news!

As we return to the parable, the wicked servant who refused to forgive was then given over to torturers for punishment. Jesus gave the grave warning that the same will be done to us if we do not forgive one another "from [the] heart" (Matt. 18:35). So how do we follow the perfect example of Jesus with a heart-level response to his forgiveness of us? There are three steps you can take to move forward.

1. Count the debt. First, we need to *count the debt*. When you're in debt, you know the exact amount due. When paying that last balance on your school loans, you can't round down or leave off twenty-five cents. It's a precise sum. The debt has to be paid in full. This applies to our debt to Christ for our sin, but it's also true about the "debt" others rack up when they hurt us. Despite our verbal attempts to forgive, we still feel angry because we carry the loss of what is due us. Someone who owes a debt has taken from another person. We carry the loss in our hearts, and this debt must be paid for us to heal. It's only natural that we daily feel the effects of the debt.

Modern medicine has tapped into this biblical principle of the power of forgiveness with medical forgiveness therapies popping up all over. Most people can point to the physical place on their body where they carry unforgiveness—a tightness in their chest, nausea, a weight on their heart or on their shoulders. Psychologists will tell you that we physically carry emotional burdens; they are our physical responses to spiritual transactions. And harbored unforgiveness accrues interest. The longer we wait to pay off a monetary debt, the more debt interest we amass for ourselves. It's the same with debts of the heart: you feel the debt owed to you, and it builds like plaque on the arteries, leading to hardness of heart. This brings in opportunities for the enemy to work. Consider the antidote to this problem of debt due to unforgiveness in Scripture.

> Anyone you forgive, I also forgive. And what I have forgiven—if there was anything to forgive—I have forgiven in the sight of Christ for your sake, in order that Satan might not outwit us. For we are not unaware of his schemes. (2 Cor. 2:10–11)

> "Be angry, and do not sin": do not let the sun go down on your wrath, nor give place to the devil. (Eph. 4:26–27, NKJV)

These passages of Scripture point to the truth that debt from unforgiveness in our hearts builds and amasses interest. Ironically, we think holding on to debt somehow gives us vindication, but in actuality, it produces a wide-open door for the enemy to invade.

When this reality hits, our active response to unforgiveness is to get rid of the debt. But someone has to pay it and take the burden. We look to Jesus, who completely wiped the slate clean of every debt we have and will ever owe. His work on the cross took our debts from us and paid them by taking our place. His blood, in perfect fulfillment, pardoned us. So we do the same with the debts that others owe us. We pass them to Jesus, and we choose to cancel what we feel the person owes us—just like Jesus canceled what we owe him. We imitate him in this act of grace, and by canceling what was owed, we are lifted from the weight of carrying the debt.

The weight of the sum owed to us is often too heavy a burden for us to bear, and he releases us from that weight the moment we give up the burden of holding on to our debts. We give Jesus what our hearts can't carry—which the enemy wishes and hopes we will keep—and pass down the power of his forgiveness to those whom we deem undeserving. This is one of the most beautiful ways we can look like Jesus and imitate him.

2. Release judgment. Once we count the debt, pass it to Jesus, and cancel it, there is another important step to complete. Often, when we have dealt with the debt that we carry, we can still be caught in a place of judgment. Our second step in forgiveness from the heart is to deal truly with the judgment that produces a bitter root if not released. For example, we can count the list of debts that our earthly father owes us but still make judgments about his ability as a parent. Or we can forgive a friend for a litany of wrongs but still hold her to a standard she can never meet.

Even if the debt is counted and canceled, judgment can still offer the enemy a back door into the heart. So as we seek biblical forgiveness, we must actively *release judgment.* Consider the following Scriptures about this step.

> Judge not, that you be not judged. For with the judgment you pronounce you will be judged, and with the measure you use it will be measured to you. (Matt. 7:1–2, ESV)
>
> Do not judge, and you will not be judged. Do not condemn, and you will not be condemned. Forgive, and you will be forgiven. (Luke 6:37)
>
> Therefore let us not pass judgment on one another any longer, but rather decide never to put a stumbling block or hinderance in the way of a brother. (Rom. 14:13, ESV)

Have you ever been at an office party or holiday family gathering where you can feel the tension in the room, even though *no one* will say what they are thinking? It's judgment lingering in the room. Often, this judgment hangs over the gathering like a mosquito net, holding everyone captive. It is unspoken and hidden, hard to express with words, but it's felt—and felt deeply. It surfaces, though during uncomfortable conversations and awkward avoidances. No one is comfortable and no one shows vulnerability because of the tension, even though they may not be able to name it.

If we let judgment prevail, trust flees and we lose unity. The enemy thrives in this environment and desires to keep cultivating the scorn. In order to banish the enemy from our hearts, then, we must release people from our judgment.

Remember the king in the parable about the unmerciful servant? He not only canceled the servant's debt in full but he also released him. The servant no longer owed him *anything*.

Likewise, we need to release those who have wronged us from our judgment and let go of requiring them to fix the situation or resolve our pain. Even on a person's best day, they likely cannot fix the consequences of their wrongdoing. Sometimes, they have no idea of the level of pain they have caused in us. By releasing them from our judgment, we clean their slate and take them off the hook for having to be the solution to our pain. Even more, we rightfully give the role of judge back to Jesus, the only one who can hold that position in perfect balance of justice and mercy (James 4:12).

3. Allow God to fill the need. The pain we feel from past wounds is valid. A void in our heart hurts when someone was supposed to fill a God-placed need and did not. Someone neglected our needs or made them worse, but no matter how we were wounded, the wound remains and needs to be healed. It needs to be filled. By releasing the one who wounded us from our judgment, and thus the job of filling the need, we free that need to be filled by someone else. And it just so happens that the most perfect and loving being who excels at filling voids and fixing needs is the Lord.

So the last step in heart-level forgiveness is letting God do the job of healing the wound and filling the hole. We can simply acknowledge the wound to our good Father God, state that we want redemption and healing, and call out to the One who can perfectly meet the requirements—and who longs to do so. God delights in this communion of restoration and opportunity to grow our trust with him. He does this better than anyone else, and he makes us whole when we allow him access to the forgotten or bruised places in our lives. He truly does heal "the brokenhearted" when we show him the broken places (Ps. 147:3). Our God is gentle and thorough in his healing, and he is good.

PERSONAL PRAYER

1. Many of us have a need to forgive multiple people from the heart. Now that you more clearly see the truth of biblical forgiveness, you might feel overwhelmed at the responsibility of dealing with those who have hurt you. It might seem impossible to get through your list of grievances to forgive. But you can trust the Lord with it. His timing is perfect, and his ways are good.

   Begin by asking the Lord to show you where to start in making your list. You might want to make a list of everyone you feel led to forgive. That can be a helpful way to begin, and it can help clear your mind. Don't worry about naming every single person you can think of. Begin by asking God who should be on your list and write out names as the Spirit leads you, taking no longer than five minutes or so. Trust God to show you who are "most ripe" to walk forgiveness from the heart with.

   As you write your list below, first ask the Lord to show you whom he wants to start with. He knows what you need today and the person with whom you should begin the process of forgiveness from the heart.

   _____

   _____

   _____

   _____

   _____

2. Once you've finished your initial list of names, ask the Lord to help you by his Spirit to search your heart for all of the debt you carry from that person you are starting with. Name the ways you feel they owe you something or did not meet your expectations. Pray this list out loud and write it down.

As you do, depend on the Lord to show you what burdens your heart. Start by saying, "Jesus, [person's name] owes me . . ." and begin listing what they did and how they made you feel. Name what they neglected to do or the wrongs they committed that still cause you suffering.

You're making an important list, so allow yourself plenty of time to list even the smallest details or broadest wrongs. This is time well spent because you are essentially allowing the Lord to peel off debts you cannot carry. There is no shame for taking the necessary time. God gives grace to forgive from the heart, so invite the Lord to show you every place you need to account for, and then write each one down. Some examples are:

- "Jesus, my dad owes me because I never felt protected and his job was to make me feel safe."
- "Jesus, my mom owes me because she left when I was fifteen and missed my sweet sixteen and my graduation. Her new life with her boyfriend was more important, and she missed every important milestone in my teenage years."
- "Father, that time my coach mocked me in front of the team, I was mortified. I can remember like it was yesterday, and he owes me."
- "Jesus, when my wife questioned my integrity in front of the kids, I was hurt and confused. It was like she didn't see everything I was trying to do for their good. She owes me for that, and I still feel angry about it."
- "Father, my friend owes me because of how she ended our friendship. It not only hurt me but also my children and my entire household. We all had to grieve it and were confused. I had no idea how to explain it to my kids, who were shocked and sad. She owes me for that."
- "God, my brother owes me because I just always felt like he didn't like me—like I was too much for him and that he wanted our relationship

to be distant. He seemed happier with his hobbies than with me. It still makes me feel lonely, like I did something wrong, and he owes me for that."

Ask the Lord to show you the specific debts a person owes you and begin writing them down. Then pray the list out loud, sharing the list with the Lord, similar to the examples above. Remember, this debt list can include both broad items (like "she owed me safety") and specific items (like "she owed me when she took the pills and asked me not to tell anyone on that Christmas Eve"). Your items can also cover years of a certain relationship. Trust the Lord to bring to mind the examples that he wants to provide freedom in.

_____

_____

_____

_____

_____

_____

_____

_____

_____

_____

_____

3. Once you've counted outstanding debts owed you, allow God to loosen their power so you don't carry them any longer. If you did this as a cognitive exercise, it would have likely been done in your own strength, and you'll likely take the debts back again. There is something extremely freeing about passing the debt to Jesus in prayer, declaring them canceled and *no longer in your possession.* In his hands, it is up and off your heart.

Remember, you are talking to *Jesus,* who has canceled every one of your debts in full, even when you did not deserve it. So in this transaction through prayer, you are choosing to look like him—offering to someone what they don't deserve, just like he did for you. And biblically, this gets your heart out of jail. It can be as simple as saying:

> *Jesus, I pass this list to you and declare that it is canceled, just like you have canceled all of my debts. I no longer hold these things, and I trust you with them. The person who wronged me has a clean slate with me.*

Close your eyes and begin setting your mind on Jesus. How he canceled every debt you owe him. Pass to him the weighty debt list others owe you, and then declare they are canceled. Record your thoughts and emotions as you do this. Also, write any responses you sense the Lord might be offering.

_____

_____

_____

_____

_____

4. After canceling the debt, release your judgment of the person. This is important, and it can be a simple yet profound way to pray to remove the rights you may have given the enemy in your life. No longer can the enemy continue planting bitter roots that rob your peace. Your prayer of release can sound something like this:

> *Jesus, I release this person from my judgment. They are no longer the solution to my pain. I take them off the hook for having to make this right.*

Write with your own words an obedient declaration of releasing the person from your judgment and giving the role of judge back to Jesus.

_____

_____

_____

_____

_____

5. I call the next step "bonus points." Because woundings are so varied, there is not one way to get these points. Instead, you must follow the leading of the Lord to bless the person, pray for those who persecute you, love your enemies, or walk in mercy. Doing so allows for forgiveness from the heart to be sealed. You bear a wide range of wrongs even beyond what's been presented in this chapter. Some are small and not very harmful but still leave a lasting stain on your heart. Others are traumatic and unimaginable, meant to steal every morsel of peace and identity you have.

After you have canceled the debts and released the persons from your judgment, release the persons who've wronged you to Jesus with mercy or blessing. To the worst wounds, this can simply be praying mercy over the person's life or that Jesus would be "in charge of them now" and that they would know him. True forgiveness from the heart does not require a lack of boundaries or dictate that you forget; it just takes the debt off your heart.

In that free place, you have the right to speak a blessing over even your worst of enemies, to offer mercy, and to pray from a new place of freedom for someone you love and might continue to have interactions with, despite being wounded. This can look like praying:

- "Lord, can you show me what you think about this person, so I can agree with you in prayer?"
- "Can you tell me, God, who *you say* they are?"
- "Jesus, I speak mercy over this person who wronged me. I know they had no idea the damage they produced would be lasting and deep."
- "God, the indescribable harm this person inflicted on me feels over-whelming, and I release this person to you. They no longer have rights to plague my life. Have mercy on them."
- "Lord, I bless this person and ask that you pour out your favor on them despite the wrong."

As you release the person who wounded you before Jesus in prayer, pray mercy, blessing, or favor, and pray for them as his Spirit leads you. Record any impressions or responses you sense as you do this.

_____

_____

_____

6. Last, God created us with real needs and desires that are from him and meant to be met or fulfilled by others—especially in close family and friend relationships. When people who were created to meet those needs do not meet them, our needs remain. We feel the deficit and act from that deficit. Ultimately, God can and will meet the needs in perfect provision when others cannot.

So ask him to fill the places that a parent missed; to show you what it means to be covered by him as our perfect Father; to ask him to be a confidant, like a best friend; or to nurture and counsel you if important people in your life were emotionally distant. In this final step, ask him to meet the unfulfilled need the person who hurt you did not fill.

Then ask God to reveal to you specifically what you really needed from the person who wounded you, and give God the job of filling up your heart in that way. Ask him to show you what it would look like if he filled the need that was neglected in your life.

_____

_____

_____

Remember, this is the God who fills "you with all joy and peace as you trust in him, so that you may overflow with hope by the power of the Holy Spirit" (Rom. 15:13). By dealing with the debt and judgment, you've now done everything necessary to forgive from the heart. You've allowed God to pull the debt up and off you, so there is room now to be filled to overflowing! Anything that threatens to steal your peace and joy does not have a right to stay. In the same manner, this kind of forgiveness from the heart allows God to reveal his goodness to you as he prepares a table in front of your enemies and showers your head with oil (Ps. 23:5).

Praying forgiveness in this way allows you to deal with those who wronged you from the safety of his table so your cup can overflow. True forgiveness appropriates a biblical truth to allow for the darkness of debt and judgment to be removed to make space for the overflow. God's trade-in is most definitely a trade-up here, and it is profoundly and abundantly good.

COMMUNITY CONNECTION

1. Were you surprised about whom God first showed you to forgive as you developed your forgiveness list?

2. What was the hardest step in forgiveness from the heart? Counting the debt? Passing it? Canceling it? Releasing judgment? Blessing or speaking mercy? Allowing God to fill the need?

3. Share with the group why a particular step was hard. Why did you struggle there? Maybe it was a belief about yourself that isn't true or a belief about God that stunted the process of stepping into true, heart-level freedom in forgiveness.

4. Did anyone struggle with guilt as they counted the debt someone owed them? Often when counting that debt, especially with a close friend or family member, many people struggle with saying it out loud or actually acknowledging that someone "owed" them.

   Recall the parable in Matthew 18:21–35 of the king and servant. Debts matter, and they have to be paid. The purpose in counting debt is not to pass judgment or blame; rather, it is naming specific items we too often ignore. These things are present every day, just under the surface. Unfortunately, they can often get bruised by others who have no idea what they "bumped" into. Discuss with your group the struggle with guilt while counting the debt.

5. Has anyone struggled with this thought: *What if I go through the process of forgiveness from the heart, then the very next day (or hour), I feel more debt and all of those feelings return?*

   It is normal for that to happen—God always finishes what he starts, and his freedom is complete. Often, people forgive years of hurt with important relationships in layers. Just quickly walk the same steps again for that one specific layer—alone or with a friend's help. This is walking out your sanctification and actually renewing your mind as you learn a new and true way of forgiving. Eventually, with practice, you will not hold a debt much longer than a few seconds—dealing almost instinctively with it before it takes root and becomes harmful. Share with your group any worries you may have about your ability to hold on to true forgiveness from the heart.

6. Consider appropriate boundaries as you seek forgiveness from the heart. Because woundings are so diverse, those boundary lines will look different for different people. Some of us will truly forgive but need to keep strong boundaries for the sake of our emotional and even physical health. David says in Psalm 16, "Boundary lines have fallen for me in pleasant places; surely I have a delightful inheritance" (v. 6). God understands our need for pleasant boundaries and safe places.

Are boundaries a concern for members of your group? If so, ask him to show you where those boundaries are and how to walk them out. Share with your community those concerns with boundaries if they apply to you. Pray for those group members who will need to navigate setting or keeping boundaries. You can ask for specifics as they come up in your challenging relationships.

Forgiveness does not mean saying the person who wronged you is not at fault. It is acknowledging the fault clearly and precisely but not holding on to it or demanding vindication. After walking forgiveness from the heart, you must realize the person who hurt you may never change. But you have. And you have given that person a clear path for changing too—with God, in his timing and in his way. That hidden-yet-felt reality for you hovers in your relationships that previously caused pain. Because of your true forgiveness, judgment, justice, and debt are removed from you. Your heart is out of jail, and you have handed the keys to the other person—if and when they are ready for freedom with God. No matter their response, you are free and you look like Jesus in your forgiveness from the heart.

8

UNGODLY BELIEFS: THE DECAY

Guide me in your truth and teach me, for you are God
my Savior, and my hope is in you all day long.
— Psalm 25:5

Remember that trash on my field and lawn? Think about what would happen if it never got picked up and disposed of. Seemingly innocent trash can have lasting effects if left on the ground too long.

My family is a big fan of *cascarones* at Easter time. These are hollowed-out eggs painted and filled with confetti. Colorful and beautiful, but a mess! We were first introduced to these when we lived in Texas. These celebratory Easter eggs, full of paper confetti, are made to smash on other people's heads. Egg shells and tiny papers end up in hair and clothes and everywhere else. I know that sounds sort of twisted, but it is great fun!

Our family tends to have massive Easter gatherings, and those *cascarones* end up scattered all over our field. As pretty as those brightly colored, cracked eggshells are, they also seem impossible to pick up. The broken egg shells tend to nestle down in between blades of grass, along with their confetti, and stay there for months. Eventually, when it rains, the colors bleed onto the grass and sidewalk and somehow end up on my family's shoes. Then, despite my pleas for my family to take off their shoes, my rugs and hardwood floors end up having color and confetti tracked on them. We hope the eggs and color will quickly go away after Eastertime, but they only become worse. When late summer arrives, we still find evidence of those eggs!

What about other unsightly trash on the lawn? If we leave it or toss it behind a bush, it still sticks around too. Besides being a nuisance, it takes a toll on our yard. The trash stays relatively the same, but it affects the ground underneath it. The grass dies and turns yellow from that trash, and whatever was in those cans and bottles tends to smell and rot. No matter what kind of trash ends up in the field, it has a way of coloring the landscape, bringing death and stench.

WHEN FALSE BELIEFS TAKE OVER

False beliefs about ourselves and about God that we carry have a way of doing just the same, discoloring the landscape of our hearts and taking a toll that brings decay. Ungodly beliefs or lies that *feel* true but don't line up with God's truth have a way of working themselves into the landscape of who we are. They can start out innocent enough or even parade themselves as religious truth. They might even feel normal and as though they belong in our lives. Or perhaps they feel unsightly, and we have no foreseeable way of cleaning them up. In this case, we might feel at home, even if we know deep down they are binding and oppressive. Those ungodly beliefs don't match the truth and character of God and don't match Scripture, but they somehow *feel* true. We tend to act on how we feel, and over time, our beliefs tend to set up a permanent residence in our hearts.

> Remember, a lot of the trash that causes our false beliefs is often thrown there by other people.

We didn't ask for it, yet it causes pain. Then we are still left to deal with the cleanup, which is easily forgotten or ignored. In other cases, we form false beliefs subtly over time, when something good gets twisted just enough to turn sour and falsely color our understanding.

If the trash in our hearts hangs out too long, it changes our view, alters our persuasions, and ultimately threatens our identity—and not for the good. If the enemy comes to steal, kill, and destroy, you can bet he will happily use decaying trash as an apparatus for his destruction in our lives.

THE VIEW OF THE OLDER BROTHER

The older brother in the prodigal son parable in Luke 15 is the clearest example in Scripture of what happens if we don't attend to seemingly "normal" pieces of trash that don't belong. They start to change the landscape of our hearts.

When we meet the older brother in the story, he is working in the field. Most of us with ungodly beliefs—beliefs that don't match with God's truth and character—are workers by nature. We strive and believe that somehow our worth and acceptance are tied to what we do. But that is a worldly system of value that ignores the surpassing greatness of what Jesus did. When the older brother hears of his brother's party, he immediately becomes angry and bitter. The lie has decayed his heart long enough over time, so now he believes his brother is taking *his* birthright too.

In his indignation, the older brother's reaction to his father is quick and telling: "What about me?" The forgotten "trash" has in fact rotted and now surfaced fully. He quickly lists his works—how he has slaved for years and never disobeyed his father. He bemoans that his father has never given him a young goat so he can have a party with his friends. The lies of being forgotten, taken for granted, and being overlooked decomposed over years in his heart, whether or not he was aware of it. The good news is his father quickly changes the landscape back to what is true about his identity.

He says what each of us needs to hear in moments like these, when lies feel true and our identity goes missing in a sea of garbage washing up on the shore. I love how the father in this story replaces lies with truth, so efficiently and straight to the heart with exactly what the older brother needs to hear.

The good father reminds him of his true identity by saying, "My son" (v. 31). Despite the garbage in his son's heart, the father tells him the truth about who he is and how he isn't actually slaving away. He has asked the son to labor joyfully alongside *as an heir*, not a slave:

> With an inheritance. With benefits.
> With relationship. As a son.

Next, he says, "You are always with me" (v. 31). While the son had chosen to work in the field during a celebration, the father now invites him back onto the property. Near to him. Back to the place from which those lies had moved him away—away from the father. He calls his son to change the proximity of their relationship. He essentially says, "I am inviting you to take your rightful position next to me as cohost of the party!"

Finally, he says, "Everything I have is yours" (v. 31). The calf the son wanted, he could have that and more. The son has a vast abundance of good given by his father, and every word the father speaks tries to replace the lies with very specific truth. The father's message is, "I will give you anything I have—you just need to ask."

Do you see how those lies lay there just ready to explode when the older brother felt slighted? His younger brother's return did not place the lies there; they revealed them. That's how trash on our lawn works. Left long enough, it will be exposed, and the long-term damage will be noticed. Often it will be noticed by people who weren't responsible for placing it there.

The father was on the receiving end of his son's exposed trash, but he was not responsible for it. He was met with an explosion of lies that could no longer stay dormant. But for him and for us, no matter how long the trash has been there, our perfect Father God's remedy is the same. He speaks the truth about our identity, he draws us close to him, and he invites us out of that spiritually desolate field to all we could ever ask for or imagine. For every problem caused by untruth, the solution is nearness to God. For every fear, false identity, jealous thought, disconnection, and bitter feeling, the remedy is being close to God as a son or daughter.

> *For every problem caused by untruth, the solution is nearness to God.*

PERSONAL PRAYER

1. Ask the Lord to show you where in your life "the trash" has caused decay. Don't feel condemnation if you have some ungodly beliefs about God that don't match the truth of how he thinks and responds to you. We all have them. God knew how easily we could be deceived and so, in his grace, gave us the Spirit.

> But when He, the Spirit of truth, comes, He will guide you into all the truth; for He will not speak on His own, but whatever He hears, He will speak; and He will disclose to you what is to come. (John 16:13, NASB)

Knowing we have holy help to uncover lies and replace them with truth is a relief.

Ask the Holy Spirit to show you where you have believed something false about who he is or his love for you. Some examples are:

- "God is only interested in the super-spiritual people. He doesn't have time for me."
- "God is angry at me, and I cannot get close to him."
- "God is disappointed in me and doesn't want relationship."
- "God is too busy with way more important things than the issues in my life."
- "God is distant and unconcerned with my problems."
- "God is waiting to punish me when I mess up, so I'm scared of him and avoid him."

Write any ungodly beliefs about God as he reveals them to you.

_____

_____

_____

_____

_____

_____

2. As the Lord reveals false beliefs, ask him to show you the truth about each one. This may be a verse that suddenly reveals itself like never before, a gentle quiet word from him, or even a picture in your mind that represents truth. You may get an impression about his response. Welcome all forms of his response as good. It is his glory on display to speak a truth to you that you couldn't receive without him. It is worth waiting for and seeking after. Write down any truth that the Lord shows you.

_____

_____

_____

_____

_____

3. Once you discern some of your false beliefs about God, ask him to show you any lies you believe about yourself. Ask him to name them for you. Writing them down can be helpful, as several may lend themselves to one theme, while others may reveal intentional purposes that bring specific decay. Some examples are:

- "I am not lovable."
- "I will never be successful in the Christian life."
- "I am not holy enough to be close to God."
- "I will always be forgotten."
- "I just can't do anything right."
- "All I am good for is to be taken advantage of. I'd rather be a doormat than be alone."
- "I'm done trying so hard. I will never arrive in my relationship with God."
- "I have to be perfect to be loved."

As you wait on the Lord, list the ungodly beliefs that you believe about yourself.

---

4. As ungodly beliefs about your identity surface, you are not left on your own to determine the solution. In 2 Corinthians 10:5, Paul gives the weapon of God's Word—which is living and active—showing that God knows your need to trade lies for truth. Paul says, "Destroy arguments and every lofty opinion raised against the knowledge of God, and take every thought captive to obey Christ" (ESV). How freeing to name the false beliefs, and then take them captive! Make them prisoners to what God says is true.

We are not unarmed and helpless. By definition, the enemy is a liar and a deceiver, and God offers us truth against every lie. We are prone to believe lies, but if we take them captive, we allow him to lead us to truth.

These truths are just as important to write down as the lies you believe. Remember the wealth of truth the father gave to the older brother: "My son . . . you are always with me, and everything I have is yours" (Luke 15:31). Write down the truths that counter your ungodly beliefs so you can receive them (daily if possible) and allow the Lord to renew your mind. If you struggle to hear the truth in place of the lie, search the Scriptures to remind yourself of what God says is true. You can also ask him the following:

- "Where did that lie come from?"
- "What is the root of this lie?"
- "Where did I learn that ungodly belief about you, God? About myself?"

List the truths that God gives to replace your ungodly beliefs. Add any insight that he gives about the roots of those false beliefs. They always exist for a reason, and your good Father's glory is on display when he gives revelation about the origin of those lies.

UNGODLY BELIEF	ROOT	TRUTH

COMMUNITY CONNECTION

1. As you allowed the Lord to search your heart for the ungodly beliefs and false narratives that you hold, what was your overriding emotion as you began that process? How did you feel when the process was complete?

2. Which category of false beliefs do you tend to have more of: ungodly beliefs about God or ungodly beliefs about yourself? Why do you think that is? Can you identify the root of those beliefs?

3. Did your ungodly beliefs take root because of a person or a significant event? Or did the lies form subtly over a long period of time, reinforced by many people and events?

4. Did your ungodly beliefs have a theme or thread? Sometimes naming the overarching thread is helpful to be able to wage war against the ungodly belief in the future. If we can see the lie coming, then fighting against it is easier because we can name it, define it, and often know how it causes decay.

5. As a group, bless one another in those new truths that God gave in exchange for the lies from your Personal Prayer section, and then ask him for greater awareness of his truth against any future onslaught of ungodly beliefs. Pray for one another to keep the specific truths you discussed and to have the ability to stand firm when the lies feel true. Power exists for us through communal intercession. Thank God for his kindness in revealing what keeps you bound and dulls the light you are meant to display.

The enemy knows our weaknesses and will often attempt to snuff out the truth of God about our identity. We each have a specific way in which we've been made in the image of God, which is his thumbprint on our life and how we display him in the world. Ungodly beliefs or lies are intended to distort this image, and then ultimately destroy it. Realizing the ungodly beliefs is a practical step in securing and protecting his true image in us. God has equipped us to take captive every thought that raises itself up against his truth and to run to him with each one. When we take captive those thoughts before God, he delights to deal with the lies and offer truth. God deals victoriously with the thought, receives us, and makes us whole.

9

ENTANGLEMENT: THE VINES

My eyes are ever on the LORD, for only he
will release my feet from the snare.
— Psalm 25:15

Remember how the field on my land backs up to a creek and tree line? The trees that line the creek are a few stories tall, beautiful, and full of green leaves in springtime. Around April, all of the bushes and plants, which also line the creek, blossom seemingly overnight, as the tall oaks burst into a canopy.

Green vines, however, rapidly grow along the creek bed. Full of thick green leaves, these vines begin taking over the landscape, devouring smaller bushes. Winding vines quickly swallow up stately tree trunks and intertwine themselves into extended branches. At first, the vines don't look all that menacing. We get excited when they sprout and sort of blend in with the other plants coming back to life after winter. They look green and lifelike, but we know how quickly they can choke out everything else.

Recently, as our family trimmed the creek line, we tugged and pulled, and used a chainsaw to rid our beloved trees of those vines. I even got a sore shoulder from pulling a jumbled knot of vines out of a tree! The knot was the size of a grocery cart, and the vines extending from it were eighteen feet long. Let's just say, the vines did not give up easily.

THE SHEEP AND THE SHEPHERD

Spiritual entanglements look and feel much the same. They grab our attention and seem inviting—even life-giving—but before we know it, we are tangled up in them. Most of the time, we are nearly choked out before we realize that we've stumbled into something we cannot get out of due to our curiosity or ignorance. We are stuck, and we hope for rescue.

Luke 15:1–7 tells about a shepherd who left his flock to look for a lost sheep. The sheep didn't wander out of rebellion but because of simple sheep-like curiosity or distraction. A stray sheep cannot find its way back home. In the animal kingdom they are the worst at getting out of trouble and back to safety. A skilled shepherd knows this, and when he finds his sheep, he lifts it from danger and puts the sheep on his shoulders—where the sheep can see the loneliness and mess of the place in which it had been stuck.

> On the shoulders of the shepherd, the sheep now has the shepherd's vantage point.

The shepherd bears the weight of the sheep's wandering and carries him back to the flock. The situation in Luke 15 likely looked the same. The sheep could rest securely on the strong shoulders of the shepherd as the shepherd brought it back home out of danger.

To extend the metaphor to us as people, not only can a lost person see where they were entangled, but they can see what surrounded the entanglement, how each step moved them farther from home, and how each seemingly safe step off the beaten path led to a trap. Now, from the higher view on the shepherd's shoulders, they can see their situation as it truly was. What looked inviting and good was actually going to choke them out, isolate them, and ultimately lead to destruction.

The realization that Jesus bears the weight of his sheep when we accidentally get lost—the dirt, bruises, and bad decisions that we experience when we wander all alone—is profound. The loneliness of our entanglements most often teaches us the necessary lessons we need. Being lost and snared is horrifying. Yet the shepherd returns us right into the middle of a flock again. We don't have to pay for this restored position or to prove our worth, but we are enveloped by the flock and placed among them by the very hands of a very Good Shepherd.

LURED AND LOOSED

What if every time we ended up entangled and lost, we knew our shepherd would come? What if, in the mix of our curiosity and ignorance, we knew he would rescue us and cut through every vine that threatened to choke us out—and with his own hands too? When what we do, what we say, or what we inherit generationally tangles us up in ways we don't want to be caught, we need the shepherd's rescue and we need to know that his rescue is full of grace. When we struggle in our independence to free ourselves and only find ourselves tangled up all the more, we have to trust the shepherd.

When we stumble into emotional affairs, physical affairs, agreements with darkness or cultish practices, vows or hurtful self-curses, addictions, and controlling codependent relationships that step out of God's best—his heart in all these situations is to rescue us. When we open doors that lead to unwanted consequences or when we live in generational patterns that feel normal to us but slowly creep up and devour holiness in our lives like vines,

> Jesus is the shepherd searching and looking to untangle us from what has snared us.

No one searches on social media looking for an old high school love in hopes of ruining their marriage. No one starts drinking socially in hopes of destroying their life with alcoholism. No one gets tied to a person in such a way that they hope they can no longer think for themselves. No one makes seemingly harmless vows to an organization, expecting to be tormented by them. No one grows up hoping to repeat the dysfunctional patterns of their family but discovers that they are doing the very same things they hated.

Yes, we must repent. Yes, we have to want to get untangled. But often we get in over our heads and desperately need to be carried by the only One who is head over it all. We need his hands to untie us, to pick us up, to place us on his shoulders, and to carry us back to the flock. We cannot do it on our own.

Our words matter. They have the ability to bring either life or death (Prov. 18:21; Matt. 12:33–37). The law of reaping and sowing is legitimate and plays out legally in our lives, sometimes without our even realizing it is in motion. Often, we get entangled by what we say, what we agree with, and what we vow. Like creeping vines, our words can determine our course over time. Our words can snare us and keep us tied, but Jesus, the best shepherd, bears the weight of our consequences and holds the power to sever even the tightest knots that we find ourselves caught in. He owns the flock, he endears himself to the flock, and he looks for us long before we cry out for rescue. He starts looking the moment we are no longer in his view.

THE DECEPTION OF DESIRE

Once my family battled our way through cutting off the beautiful vines from the trees in our backyard, those vines didn't look so pretty after all. Vines need the structure of the tree and branches to have shape, and without the trees, they just look like a lifeless bundle of tangled mess.

Sometimes our spiritual entanglements disguise themselves as good, and they masquerade as our identity. We start believing the knotted mess is who we are and what we were made for. But those are lies. Anything that entangles us and draws us away from God, away from our community, and away from whom we are made to be is bondage. Christ came to set us free. We do not have to be "burdened again by a yoke of slavery," which is bent on choking the life out of us (Gal. 5:1). We can cry out to Jesus who is already out looking for us, ready to lift us up and walk us out of the mess into which we stumbled. In the end, those entanglements don't stand a chance against our Redeemer.

> *Christ came to set us free.*

PERSONAL PRAYER

1. Ask the Lord to show you where you're currently entangled. Most often, entanglements come from what began as an ignorant or curious decision, believing that a danger did not pose a threat. Consider Luke 15 again. Entanglement isn't a lost coin or a prodigal son, but someone somewhere in between. Maybe you're entangled with some sin or wounding, but in denial or unaware of the consequences of who or what you've tied yourself to. Internal vows, spoken and unspoken, often open a door to entanglement. Even a harmless-sounding statement, said over and over again, can create a tie that binds us. Statements like, "I'm so awkward," or, "I'll never have close friends," said over a lifetime can be our entrapment.

   Other times, we slip into entanglements. Emotional affairs, codependent friendships, and controlling or manipulative parent-child relationships—these are all examples of entanglements that we can get caught in. Secret societies, spiritual or new-age practices (even though they might seem biblically founded), superstitious traditions, and familiar generational patterns can easily anchor us to something unholy.

   Ask the Lord to reveal the areas of entanglement that have entrapped you previously or that currently have you bound, then list them below. These could be spoken vows or curses, relationships that are out of your marriage covenant or that hold more weight than they should. Keep in mind that addictions and anything that dictates your thoughts or actions qualify as entanglements.

   _____

   _____

   _____

   _____

   _____

2. As you look at the items on your list above, ask God to show why they hooked you. What lie initially caused you to get entangled? What was the deficit in your heart when you became tied to something unholy? Start listing the reasons you were pulled into and caught by the specific entanglements you listed. Ask God to show what you were looking for in that entanglement and what you needed.

_____

_____

_____

_____

_____

_____

_____

3. Just like the sheep in Luke 15 could not find his way back to the flock, you cannot get free from entanglements without Jesus. As you look at your lists above, repent of any entanglement where you sought to be filled by a person or a thing other than God. Ask God for help and prayerfully place the finished work of the cross between you and the entanglement that hooked you.

Then actively receive his forgiveness—don't just say it but know it. He has already paid for the sin and its consequences, and his heart seeks to bring you out of its mess. His cross has victoriously dealt with the enemy who tied you up and who is bent on your destruction. Jesus carries you back to safety. Ask him to do so, and then wait on his response. Ask him what it looks like to no longer be tied to these issues.

In a posture of prayer, ask Jesus to sever those unholy ties and break the entanglements you are caught up in as you repent and place them before him. Declare that you are no longer tangled up and tied to them because of the cross. You are tied to Jesus. You are allowing him to appropriate his victorious power and separate you from the snare. Wait for his truth about what your freedom looks like untied from the person or thing, and then rest in the comfort of his grace and forgiveness. Allow your heart permission to look to him and record any impressions or truths that he gives.

_____

_____

_____

COMMUNITY CONNECTION

1. One of the most precious truths about the lost sheep is that the shepherd brings him home and celebrates with friends. Home isn't alone in a crate somewhere but back in the flock. When we're coming out of entanglements, shame often wants to share in the homecoming too. The quickest way to usher shame out of our lives, though, is to be reminded of grace. We all know what it's like to get entangled.

   If you're willing, share with your flock about a past or current entanglement, and then let them surround you with love and grace, just like a sheep being placed right back in the center of the flock. Community is a grace and a weapon against shame.

2. A key to avoid repeating a past entanglement is to know what drew us there in the first place. Often our ignorance or curiosity led us down a dangerous path, but what kept us there was an ungodly belief. Be sure to discuss and pray together in a culture of honoring one another, which may require that mixed gender groups split into male and female groups for this topic in order to guard the subject matter appropriately.

   Share with the group some of the false narratives that kept you entangled. If you're unsure of how you became entrapped or which belief sent you wandering, ask Jesus for his perspective. Ask your friends to ask too. Remember, Jesus picks you up and places you on his shoulders. From that safety and height, you can share his vantage point and perspective. Ask him what belief allowed you to be ensnared.

3. Spend time agreeing with God in prayer to cut your ties with entanglements, to carry the burden, and to return to community. Pray for one another about specific entanglements and relish the freedom from guilt and shame that comes from exposing the lies to the light.

4. If someone in your group has been affected by a loved one's entanglements, pray as a group for one another about these situations. If any of your group members had to pick up the pieces of a close friend's addiction, a spouse's affair, or a child who has chosen an unholy path, prayerfully cover them. These can be devastating, and we can carry resulting consequences and shame with us, often unknowingly. Help your group members cut ties with any secondary unholy attachments as well as the resulting shame and guilt.

> Entanglements normally fall into three categories: 1) What we say; 2) what we do; and 3) what we inherit. Good news! Jesus has the victory over all of these and can silence the accusation of "it will always be this way." We cannot personally untangle ourselves from the vines. When we try to do this in our own strength, we often end up in worse shape. Only through God's grace can we be free. Allow him to cut you free from what binds you, and then to bring you back into the fold.

10

SIN: THE WEEDS

For if you live according to the flesh, you will die; but if by the Spirit you put to death the misdeeds of the body, you will live.

— Romans 8:13

Walking around the acres of land around my house brings rest and peace into my busy life. The land is green, and the trees provide a beautiful canopy. The creek flows over rocks, and a stately magnolia tree blooms in front of the house. Rose and hydrangea flowers emerge from the bushes, and everything seems right with the world when I trod around our land. That is, except in our newly mulched beds.

In these flowerbeds, little green weeds inevitably pop up each year. I see the weeds and pretend they aren't there. Truth be told, it only takes an extra five minutes to pull them out and discard them. That is, when they first start showing up. But I deny their presence and try to ignore them. I use time management as my excuse. Over time, however, my lawn gets covered. At that point, I can no longer take care of it myself. I have to spend time and money for professional help.

PULLING THE WEEDS

Our flesh works the same way. It requires our daily and diligent maintenance to keep it from taking over. We all adhere to patterns and habits on a daily basis, some of which are good, like brushing our teeth, taking a shower, and washing the dishes. These help us maintain our home and body. In the same way that daily drawing near to God fills us up, we must daily put to death sin that attempts to destroy our spirits. Often the weeds of sin slowly take over, and when we realize this, we attempt to cover them up and hide. Then we painstakingly try to pull all the weeds out on our own.

Jesus knows our pride in denying the weeds and he knows our frailty when they suddenly take over. We already discussed the older brother from Luke 15, but now let's focus on the prodigal son from the same parable with his propensity toward rebellion and corruption. We know how the story starts and we rejoice in the ending, but I find myself thinking about the middle, when the prodigal was making daily decisions in the weeds.

The middle of the story depicts him sitting in a pigsty when he comes to the reality of his situation and the choice either to stay or to go home. When did the prodigal realize the weeds in his life—which he had ignored, accepted, and even embraced—had taken over? When did he accept that living according to the flesh was not so exciting anymore? Did his debauchery beckon to him loudly enough to drown out remorse? What changed his mind? Each morning in his hangover and filth, did he weigh the possibilities of squashing his pride and begging forgiveness from his father? Eventually he reached the end of his rope and returned home, worried at the reception he would receive.

We all have had prodigal moments (or seasons) if we're honest. We might not call them by that name, and we might try really hard to deny our sin, but deep down we know we're rebelling against God. The sin seems better, easier, safer, more alluring, or even more productive, but we know it's still sin. Though the sin makes more noise than rational thought, it wears the guise of truth, even though it's a lie.

When we realize we are in over our heads, the last place we choose to run is home. We desperately want to be home, but we cannot fathom a response so good and so merciful as the response that God gives. So we, like the prodigal, rewrite the storyline to make God into a cruel and punishing person. We imagine his rejection and disappointment in us over and over again. But in truth, our sin is the one issuing the punishment, not God, and God's response is far from cruel. His response is better than we could ever ask for or imagine.

> If only we will go home to experience it.

The father in the prodigal son story did not hide in embarrassment over his son's rebellion. He looked and waited. When he saw his wayward son coming home from a distance, he ran to him, threw his arms around him, and kissed him. The sheer indecency and wild affection the father had for his son shakes me to my core. You know that his neighbors were watching—*they always are*—and snickering at this old man running with his skirts in his hands toward his son.

Perhaps they were gossiping the minute the father wrapped his arms around his foul-smelling and squalid son. Yet the merciful father called for the son to be covered by a robe and to have a ring for his finger and sandals for his feet. The son had not even taken a bath from his time in the pigsty, but the father called for the best robe to be placed on him. Maybe the father's eyes were misty with tears as he kissed his lost son, examining his face underneath the grime for signs of life and hope, grieving every dark night and every tossed-away truth as if he had lived it himself. Parents can feel a child's pain as if they lived it too. The son barely uttered his confession of wrong and unworthiness before the father jumped into action and planned a party.

When we run to the Father covered in our own sin, our turning to him and humble confession propel our Father toward us. He is always looking for his lost ones, waiting to cover their sin with the best robe. That best robe represents God's righteousness (Isa. 61:10). Even on the day we feel the most spotless, we cannot earn that robe. Jesus Christ purchased our robe of righteousness on the cross. It looks like Jesus in every way, and when the Father sees us in that robe, he sees Jesus. The prodigal received a ring on his finger—a sign of sonship restored. He didn't have to earn back trust or work for the right to have it. It was freely given.

Finally, the shoes on his feet signify that despite the son's begging to be a servant, he was indeed a son. While servants in those days worked barefoot, sons wore shoes and sat at the table. No amount of sin could have erased the son's identity and inheritance. And not only did he get a seat at the table, but he also received a glorious feast and celebration in honor of his return. This is the heart of Father God, his response every time we come limping back home, full of guilt and shame. This is truth.

> *God is always looking for his lost ones.*

We might want to rewrite the storyline or change the ending, but God's holiness demands his consistency. We're tempted to believe it works for others but surely not for us. Yet he responds to all of us the way the father responded when the prodigal came home. This was and always is an act of mercy that far outweighs our expectation of judgment.

Jesus left us at the end of this story to ponder and earnestly decide if we believe the truth of God's mercy. So often in our sin, we hide from the help of our good Father. We dig our grave deeper and deeper, believing the casket of sin is our new home and destiny. That is not what we were made for.

> He invites us all to come back home
> and be restored.

IN THE LIGHT AND LOVED

A few times as a parent, I have watched my children hide from me out of guilt or shame. They have done this over even the smallest of wrongs because they sometimes believe I might respond in a certain way. But they are believing a lie. When they finally confess their wrong, my response is almost always love, grace, and help. I'm far from perfect, but having sat with many prodigals in prayer times, I am acutely aware my response as a parent needs to reflect the Father's response—and when it doesn't, I create a chasm between my children and their perception of God as parent.

On those less-than-perfect days, I feel the Lord's check on my heart when my kneejerk reaction wants to make my children really feel my disappointment and anger. I eventually and intentionally pivot from anger to grace, knowing that when I do, I shape not only our future relationship but also their idea of the grace in confession. I will often remind them of my response afterward, asking, "Was I mad? Did I get angry? Did I yell? Did I shame you?" just so they can remember what is true for next time.

Yes, often there are consequences for children to face, but consequences should fit the crime—and often they are just the direct results of their action or inaction. In the end, if we as parents reflect the Father's response to sin with our receiving of them and immediate restoration, then we remind them of who they really are in the middle of the guilt that shrouds them. This is how we embrace them in their shame and fear and usher them back to their true identity. Modeling what the father displayed in Luke 15 is the goal: that I am waiting to accept them without the shameful in between of demanding they grovel and earn it all back.

While I sometimes fail in this, I am committed to fixing it and responding in a way that reflects God's love. In the moments I might miss it as a parent, I am struck by the overwhelming love of God. His response is so perfect, so true, so humble, and so good. No other god responds like this. His love is life changing. Consider this truth from Ephesians:

> But because of his great love for us, God, who is rich in mercy, made us alive with Christ even when we were dead in transgressions—it is by grace you have been saved. (Eph. 2:4–5)

We were dead in our sins and given life back. Like the prodigal who came home with rags and was restored with a robe, ring, and sandals back to sonship, when we turn from sin and acknowledge the wrong, we are met with mercy. "Whoever conceals their sins does not prosper, but the one who confesses and renounces them finds mercy" (Prov. 28:13).

At this point in my faith journey, I don't struggle confessing my sin to God. I understand, at least on some level, his grace that was purchased for me. Confessing to other people seems to come with a higher risk, though. I notice this to be true for countless others as well. Admitting my worst sins and skeletons in the closet to other people is scary and vulnerable. Yet I experience great liberation in confessing to others as well as to God. As the apostle John writes, "If we walk in the light, as he is in the light, we have fellowship with one another, and the blood of Jesus, his Son, purifies us from all sin" (1 John 1:7).

> *When we turn from sin and acknowledge the wrong, we are met with mercy.*

When friends confess their darkest secrets and worst moments to me, my fellowship with them increases exponentially. I love them all the more, advocate for their freedom with greater measure of fervency, and treasure their vulnerability even more, because I know the risk they felt in telling me. It is the same risk I took by sharing with them.

In our culture that thrives on performance and platform, how upside down is it that confessing our worst possible deeds and thoughts actually opens the door to the community we crave? When we open our mouths in front of others, we not only get fellowship, but we get purification. We long for both and we crave both. Something about placing our darkness into the light removes sin from us and surrounds us with those who cheer us on to freedom.

What a glorious position—to be on the receiving end of God's rich mercy and to be offered the gift of grace through confession. In the middle of our blubbering admittance of wrong, we receive the sweetest gift of being wrapped in the arms of the One who never stopped looking, who never gave up on us. He offers us his never-ending mercy that is always new and abundant.

PERSONAL PRAYER

1. Ask the Lord to reveal to you the places in your life where you are currently choosing the prodigal's path, even in the smallest of sins. As he reveals these, place them back before him. Get up close to him and confess that you have agreed with the lie associated with these sins, but that you no longer want to partner with these lies bent on your destruction. As the Lord reveals those areas of sin, confess them, both big and small.

_____

_____

_____

_____

_____

2. Ask the Lord to show you why these particular sins have a foothold in your life. When did they start to grip you? Where did they come from? What we falsely believe about ourselves or God can lead us down an unrighteous path. Often, it's a particular reason that sin has power over you, so ask the Lord, who knows and longs to be gracious to you, to reveal that reason to you. As you listen to the Lord, consider the hold and allure of each sin. List the roots of them and what you believe keeps them present in your life.

_____

_____

_____

_____

3. Finally, ask the Lord what needs to be restored. Do you need to receive fully God's forgiveness and really wear the robe of righteousness that was purchased for you? Or do you need to put on your ring to remind you that your inheritance in the kingdom of God is not lost on you? Or do you need to receive the sandals to accept that you are truly a son or daughter of God, despite where you previously felt in bondage? Ask the Lord to remind you of these birthrights and to restore the pieces that feel lost due to sin. As you wait, list by name those areas of your life where you want restoration.

_____

_____

_____

COMMUNITY CONNECTION

1. As a community, be brave among one another to confess your sins (if appropriate in your group setting or in same gender groups if necessary). Say what you don't want to say, and watch what happens when you do. Feel the weight lift off your chest and bask in the light that sin removed from you. Look into the eyes of those around you and celebrate that you don't have to harbor secrets anymore.

2. After someone in the group confesses sin, spend time agreeing with God in his mercy and restoration. Pray over each one who confesses. Ask the Lord to show you what his robe, ring, and sandals look like for the one who puts their sin into the light. Celebrate each friend who has now turned from their sin and come back home to the Father like the prodigal did. Reflect God's response in what you pray, say, and do.

3. If some people in your group are in the middle of rebellion, ask God to reveal to them false beliefs they hold about him that are keeping them from running home to their Father. Do they believe he is ashamed of them? That he is forever angry with them? That they won't be welcomed back into the household of God?

   Spend time together in prayer waiting on God to reveal his truth in their situation and use the father's response in Luke 15 as the gauge for his truest heart toward them. To those in the middle of a rebellion, God is looking, waiting, and can see you coming from far away. His embrace is full, his covering complete, and his restoration the sweetest of gifts.

When God looks at us, he sees his sons and daughters no longer defined by their sin. When he looks at us, he sees Jesus, his Son, who paid every debt we owe. We must truly confess and repent of our sin, but once we do, we no longer wear it as our identity and we're no longer obligated to obey it. Our flesh doesn't dictate our decisions. As sons and daughters led by the Spirit, our identity is not shaky. It is secure as heirs (Gal. 4:7).

11

WARFARE: THE BATTLE

The Lord has broken through my enemies
before me like the breakthrough of waters.
— 2 Samuel 5:20, NASB

For the first fourteen years of our marriage, I was a military wife with my husband serving in the Air Force. I remember receiving random phone calls from military personnel asking me, "Are you all secure?" I was educated early that the answer to that question and those like it was vitally important. It was code for, "Is everyone accounted for? Is everyone safe? Is everyone where they are supposed to be?" In the military, even in times of peace, you are assumed to be combat-ready even if you are not engaged in combat. The military expected—and occasionally called—to verify that readiness.

In Scripture, we find a similar stance promoted again and again in over one hundred verses. These verses depict spiritual warfare and combat readiness, and they describe the tactics of our enemy in detail. Warfare is common, and it is assumed that we will engage in it more often than not. Consider a few examples.

> Submit yourselves, then, to God. Resist the devil, and he will flee from you. (James 4:7)
>
> For though we live in the world, we do not wage war as the world does. The weapons we fight with are not the weapons of the world. On the contrary, they have divine power to demolish strongholds. (2 Cor. 10:3–5)

> Be of sober spirit, be on the alert. Your adversary, the devil, prowls around like a roaring lion, seeking someone to devour. So resist him, firm in your faith. (1 Pet. 5:8–9, NASB)

These verses describe a very real battle that occurs in the spiritual realm, and each one of us is an integral participant.

Yet many of us walk our daily Christian life in a fog, not recognizing our unseen reality, although still affected by it. We don't live a combat-ready lifestyle—and often, we don't care to live like that. It would force us to deal directly with the two teams in the battle. Many of us struggle even to come near to God, although we know we should. And we certainly do not even want to think about the enemy. Denial feels safer, and we often choose to remain ignorant to the warfare around us—out of fear, out of arrogance, or simply because to engage in battle would cost us too much.

THE SPIRITUAL WAR ALL AROUND

From the opening pages of Scripture, we see a battle waging and opponents on each side. God gave Adam a measure of control, and when he and Eve were deceived by Satan and acted in rebellion, mankind became subject to the schemes of Satan and his demons. During his ministry on earth, Jesus cast out demons regularly and instructed his disciples to cast out demons too. They were sometimes found doing so in the synagogues, or our equivalent of the church. When Jesus died, descended, rose from the grave, and ascended, Satan and his demons were completely disgraced. They no longer carried authority over God's children.

While Jesus is currently at the right hand of God, his return will establish his ultimate authority and reign. Until then, Satan has a measure of control for a limited period of time, and he will go to great lengths to distort, accuse, steal, kill, and destroy as much as possible before Jesus returns and he faces his doom.[4]

Most of us are familiar with those two opponents in battle. We've read the stories, and quite honestly, many of us like to skip over the stories about demons being cast out because they can make us afraid or uncomfortable. But the enemy already wins the battles each time we choose to ignore them. He also wins when we merely bookend our understanding of a spiritual battle with the two main opponents and withdraw our involvement from the story.

> When we remove our role in spiritual warfare, we remove our power.

We are a third party in this war (yet on the winning team for sure), and we can carry victory over the enemy by the power of Jesus. We—as Christians and as a church—were meant to partner with God in this battle. We have the victory! We are free from the decree of death that Satan promotes, and we were designed to act on the offensive under that authority that was purchased by Jesus.

One of our main roles as the church is to give evidence to the unseen of God's wisdom: "Through the church, the manifold wisdom of God should be made known to the rulers and authorities in the heavenly realms" (Eph. 3:10). We were made to be a demonstration in the battle, and a victorious one at that. We carry the Spirit of God, have been given weapons of warfare, and have been given the ability to exist in a combat-ready status. Spiritual pacifism is not a safe posture; it is a death sentence because there is no neutral ground in spiritual warfare.

Let me pause here to acknowledge that this topic has the ability to make people wildly uncomfortable. If you fall into that category, there is no shame. If you feel like you aren't knowledgeable or that the way you were raised negatively affects your thoughts on this topic, I encourage you to press through with a heart open to what the Lord may want to offer. This topic is important to him, as shown by the many spiritual warfare verses in Scripture.

As followers of Jesus, we often find ourselves in one of two ditches when it comes to spiritual warfare: One ditch decides that everything is a battle, where demons are hiding under every rock and every circumstance that does not fit our personal definition of how the Lord would do it is an outright attack. We label consequences of presumptuous,

> *There is no neutral ground in spiritual warfare.*

willful, and ignorant sin as the enemy, subtly dismissing personal ownership on our part in the chaos that follows. The other ditch denies the existence of demons and, in that denial, promotes a false safety in the non-existence of an enemy who prowls looking for someone to devour (1 Pet. 5:8). Both are dangerous ditches that we often find ourselves falling into. There is a third place to stand in the topic of warfare that is demonstrated beautifully in the story of David and the Philistines.

INTERACTING WITH GOD IN SPIRITUAL BATTLE

In 2 Samuel 5:17–25, David went to war against the Philistines. He had just been anointed as king over Israel, and the Philistines sought him out—and not with congratulations or gifts. It is worth noting that David had just stepped into a new seat of God-appointed authority, and that the enemy wasted no time seeking a fight. When David heard of the Philistines' advancement, he "went down to the stronghold" (v. 17).

A stronghold is a place of refuge, the means of protection in an attack. It is defined as a fortress holding safely.[5] In ancient times, a "stronghold" was a fortified wall or fortress-like city. In the Bible, God also declared himself a stronghold (Zech. 2:4–5; 2 Sam. 22:3; Ps. 9:9). "Stronghold" is also used by Paul to describe our posture in spiritual warfare (2 Cor. 10:4).

We can assume that when David went down to the stronghold, he was physically protected and spiritually able to meet in safety with the Lord. He did not cower or deny the possibility of a fight, neither did he go charging ahead. He physically went to the stronghold and inquired of the Lord (v. 19). That stronghold was a place that had been fortified prior to the attack. Fortress-like walls are not built overnight; they are planned and executed before battle.

SEVEN STEPS IN SPIRITUAL WARFARE

David's very first responses in this passage about physical warfare show us how to take our first steps in spiritual warfare. As I describe his next steps, note how David continued to interact with God in the battle.

1. Be alert. Warfare is inevitable, and sometimes we are targeted in new seasons of life or when we're given new authority. Remember, David had just been promoted into a new place of authority, and the battle followed quickly after. If I were the enemy, I would purposely scheme to attack God's people at these pivotal times and make it count. When the stakes are higher and energy and focus are placed in the new season, the enemy can easily pounce. The timing is not only when you least expect it, but it also has the potential to cause greater turmoil and affect more people if you're in a place of new authority.

I have prayed with many people who are overseas missionaries. It is uncanny to me how the enemy attacks swiftly and without mercy the moment they step on to foreign soil. It is to the enemy's advantage to disrupt when it really matters. Those missionaries had years of previous peace following Jesus, but the moment they took a focused stand for the gospel in their new culture, chaos followed. It is not a formula by any means, but there is a biblical precedent to be mindful of warfare following a new position, promotion, or transition in your life.

Be mindful of warfare following a new position, promotion, or transition in your life.

2. Go to the stronghold immediately. The moment you "hear" of the battle (sense it, smell it, think you might be in it), go to your stronghold. Your stronghold might be the place that you've cultivated in prayer from previous chapters. It may be that strong sense of abiding with intentional time and space given to encountering God. It's personal to each individual, but you have to get there. David physically went down to a fortified wall where he knew he would be able to find the Lord's guidance. In the same way, we must fortify our own relationship with God so that in the heat of the battle it is natural and normal for us to find him.

> We cannot build a shelter during a storm.

The wind is high, the rain hits hard, and lightning threatens to strike. Our sheltered strongholds must be intentionally built prior to the heat of the battle. Our good strongholds with God have to be formed in that place of abiding, where we have learned to hear his voice and draw near to it fast. Where we have practiced the discipline of silencing all other voices and finding refuge in his voice. His Spirit cannot guide us into all truth (John 16:13) if we have not taken small steps in that leading and honed our ability to follow.

3. Fortify and prepare your stronghold in peacetime so it is ready when the battle surrounds you. David arrived at the stronghold before battle and did not make a move without first inquiring of the Lord. In our own prayer times, worship, and close communion with God, we build up those walls of security that stand strong in wartime. Our kneejerk reaction must be to go to God first, but to go there, we have to prepare prior to the battle. When shots are fired, there isn't time to build a fortress or know the security found in God. David went to a place that had long before been prepared. In order to seek God in the familiar place, to hear his voice, and to wait for his plan before we do anything else, we must have a stronghold already prepared.

4. *Ask God if the battle is yours and if you will have the victory.* David asked God specific questions about the battle. He wasn't vague but asked God what he needed to know. He asked God two things in verse nineteen:

- "Should I attack the Philistines?"
- "Will you let me win?" (CEV)

The Lord answered his very specific questions with two very certain affirmations, and David proceeded in the battle.

I often see the people of God exhausted by engaging in battles they are not meant to fight. Other times, they're worn out by presuming the time to engage is imminent. They rush into battle, but over and over again in Scripture, God does not seem hurried or anxious to go to battle.[6]

> God's timing is perfect.

Often, when we don't fortify our spiritual strongholds and rush into battle, we realize we don't have the correct plan and aren't prepared. We don't even have a stronghold built at all! We see the resulting devastation and battle wounds and wonder, *What went wrong?*

5. *Proclaim God's power in the moment of victory.* The Lord made good on his promise to David by defeating the Philistines, and immediately, David responded by proclaiming, "The LORD has broken through my enemies before me like the breakthrough of waters" (v. 20, NASB).

As David fought in that battle, he probably blocked near deathblows with his shield and fought valiantly with his sword. Yet he acknowledged the only reason for his victory was the Lord's ability to swiftly break through the enemies "like the breakthrough of waters." Like a dam that begins to break with one crack that quickly allows water to push through the whole embankment, David knew how that battle was really won. He knew that at the right time the victory of the Lord would bust open the strategy of the enemy, like pent-up waters crashing through a dam.

Too often, when we experience victory, pride comes sneaking in. So be quick to acknowledge the real Victor in warfare and look intentionally for the ways in which he specifically brought about the triumph. Proclaim them and write them on your heart.

6. Do not presume that every battle plan looks the same. In the same passage, once more the Philistines tried to fight David and his army (2 Sam. 5:22–23). And again, David inquired of the Lord. This aspect of the story is subtle but so important.

In warfare when we are dependent on a formula or strategy, we lose dependence on God. Yet his love for us demands dependence on him. He is not needy or narcissistic; he just knows that his way is the best, and he wants the best for us. When we become attached to one method of fighting spiritual warfare, we fall into a trap of just doing what worked before. There is a reason we read only about the Israelites marching around a city one time to conquer it—it was a seemingly foolish plan that required utmost trust and obedience in God's instructions (Josh. 6).

When we rely on any successful formula—believing that since it worked once, it will work again—we lose close communion with God and risk defeat because we make assumptions about God. We forfeit the best outcome and miss the fullness of his will for our lives. David did not make assumptions but inquired about the next battle, as though it were the first.

When he did, the Lord gave specific instructions that required David to see and hear spiritually in order to execute: "When you hear the sound of marching in the tops of the balsam trees, then rouse yourself, for then the LORD has gone out before you to strike down the army of the Philistines" (2 Sam. 5:24, ESV). David and his army were instructed to listen for the sound of holy marching in the tops of the trees, and then to move quickly, because the Lord had already begun to strike the enemy.

Take a minute and give some thought to this strategy. Ask yourself if your heart is inclined enough before the Lord, not only to submit to that kind of unseen plan, but also to have the faith to wait for it. Then do you presently have the spiritual ears to hear the marching of the Lord?

This battle plan would have most certainly challenged David's idea of how it should be done. It probably felt foolish to him. But David did not falter and did as the Lord commanded. The Lord struck down the Philistines again. This leads to our final step in spiritual warfare.

7. Learn submission and patience to develop the spiritual ears necessary to respond to the plan of the Lord. David had to wait over twenty years to become king of Israel. He spent time fleeing and hiding, yet simultaneously delivered the people from their enemies. He inquired of the Lord throughout his life, even for the right response at Saul's death. Under extreme pressure, David penned Psalm 63, when he longed for God's presence like one thirsty in a parched land without water. He remembered God, clung to God, and earnestly sought him, despite the stress of being pursued by those wanting him dead. He praised instead of whining and recalled God's goodness instead of bemoaning his present situation.

David's response was not accidental; like him, we learn it again and again at the stronghold with God. Warfare can come on strong, but God's presence in the stronghold is fortified and secure. In the small and big battles, we are to be found there, remembering, rejoicing, and learning to hear him clearly. He is our refuge and strength.

PERSONAL PRAYER

1. In successful spiritual warfare, we must know we are indeed spiritual beings who can hear from three sources: God, the enemy, and our own voice. Just as Jesus could hear the voice of his Father, he could hear the voice of the enemy as well (Matt. 4:3). Also consider that he had his own will (Luke 22:42). Ask the Lord to show you which voice you hear most often: the voice of the Lord, the voice of the enemy, or your own voice?

_____

_____

_____

2. As you learn to differentiate between the voices you hear besides your own—God's voice or the voice of the enemy—take some time to name the voices so you can intentionally learn the difference between them. How does the Lord sound when you feel prompted by him? Does the voice of the enemy sound peaceful? Which voice sounds the most hurried or rushed?

God's voice sounds: _____

The enemy's voice sounds: _____

3. Proverbs 23:7 states that, "For as [a man] thinks in his heart, so is he" (NKJV). You are the gatekeeper of your heart, and as such, you can choose to be in awe of God yet remain merely *aware* of the enemy. For most of us, in the moment of spiritual battle, we are very aware of the voice of the enemy, and sometimes overwhelmingly impressed by it, while God's voice feels harder to hear. Sometimes we struggle even to be aware of God's voice in the battle at all. In those moments, we lose our voice in the chaos and confusion.

As we learn what each voice sounds like, however, we can choose which one we give space to and listen to. We can even learn to silence our own thoughts and yield to God's will. As you respond to the question below, think on the truth that Christ dwells in you and that you are seated with Christ (Eph. 2:6). As you have encountered warfare, have you been impressed by God? Meaning, is he the loudest voice you hear in the battle and are your eyes fixed on him? Or has the enemy taken your focus?

If the latter, ask the Lord to show you why the enemy has consumed your thoughts in battle. Also, ask God if there is anything you are falsely believing about the power of the devil or the power of God. Then ask him to reveal how that belief took root.

_____

_____

_____

_____

_____

COMMUNITY CONNECTION

1. As you consider David's actions in 2 Samuel 5:17–25, which of the seven steps listed in this chapter are you most interested in cultivating?

2. Which step have you previously invested in and seen good fruit as a result?

3. In which step do you see a present lack in your own spiritual journey? What step seems to be most difficult as you consider your spiritual warfare history? As you share within your group, wait on the Lord together to discern the reason you struggle to grow in this step.

4. Finally, take time within your community to call out growth in specific steps that you see in one another. Give examples! This is an opportunity for exhortation and encouragement. Take time to do this together, then pray for one another about both the weak and strong steps you've discussed.

> "Finally, be strong in the Lord and in his mighty power. Put on the full armor of God, so that you can take your stand against the devil's schemes. For our struggle is not against flesh and blood, but against the rulers, against the authorities, against the powers of this dark world and against the spiritual forces of evil in the heavenly realms. Therefore put on the full armor of God, so that when the day of evil comes, you may be able to stand your ground, and after you have done everything, to stand" (Eph. 6:10–13).

12

WEAPONS: THE WAY TO VICTORY

*The weapons we fight with are not the weapons
of the world. On the contrary, they have
divine power to demolish strongholds.*

— 2 Corinthians 10:4

In my house full of children, Nerf gun wars have been some of our most epic battles. Those weapons allow the soldier to hide out and simultaneously fire on the enemy from far away with a very effective (and sometimes painful) blow. I have watched as the more mature children (and often some adult friends too!) show up to battle with elite weaponry, equipped with target accuracy tools and multiple rounds. The younger children, who are just happy to be included in the battle, step out onto the battlefield with whatever they can find and seems to be powerful. But pretend pirate swords are just no match for the Nerf N-Strike Elite SurgeFire Blaster, which is able to level a young child from a long distance in seconds!

The lesson here?

> We must have the right weaponry for the battle.

As people actively engaged in spiritual warfare, we must not fight defenselessly. We have been given spiritual weaponry to wage war on the offensive. In the world's eyes, this weaponry seems foolish, but to the spiritual man, these weapons contain strategy and power. Successful combat in spiritual warfare requires spiritual weapons, but sadly, we often try to fight with the world's ammunition. And we come up short.

INTIMACY WITH GOD

Consider the prophets, their power, and their understanding that they wielded in battle. These weapons came from a life devoted to God through walking with him regularly and consistently.

When Elijah, for example, sparred with the prophets of Baal in 1 Kings 18:19–45, he did not even dare provoke them until God clearly called him out of hiding. After three years of waiting, Elijah knew the ordained time to reveal himself for the battle and he didn't move until then. He waited yet enjoyed spiritual intimacy with the Lord during that time. Our intimacy with God is crucial for spiritual warfare.

How often do we pick a fight out of our indignance? Ill-timed and premature fights don't end well. But in 1 Kings 18 the details mattered, and the Lord's response was specific. When Elijah encountered Obadiah, it was not accidental, and when he met Ahab face-to-face the timing was perfect. The setting of the story was primed for the epic battle, with severe famine in the background and prophets hidden in caves. Chaos and a mob on Mt. Carmel set the stage for Elijah to condemn the people for wavering in their loyalty to God. It would have been easy for Elijah to have responded earlier; he was hunted and people were starving. But Elijah's spiritual GPS was honed over time as he waited on God.

> *Our intimacy with God is crucial for spiritual warfare.*

Later, when Elijah encountered the prophets of Baal, he didn't wage war with showy repetition in his prayers, and he didn't step into a costumed caricature of a hero to portray himself as a supernatural prophet. He was efficient, measured, and controlled. He didn't cater to his enemies' chaotic cries and acts of dramatic self-harm as they tried to appease their false god for fire. When Elijah called down fire, the all-consuming fire made way for holy rain. He made bold moves because he knew God's ways and God's voice. This came from a lifetime of intimacy.

Elijah had honed his use of spiritual weaponry, forged through years of knowing God. These weren't new toys for a display of impressive bravado; no,

WEAPONS: THE WAY TO VICTORY

they were weapons of warfare that fit securely and comfortably in his hands. At the end of the battle, it was not his own heroics that he wanted to display. It was God's glory and the edification of the people for which he utilized his weapons.

His ability to hear the Commander, obey the Commander, honor truth, and know exactly what weapon to wield at the appointed time—all this came from intentional intimacy with God. In the rest of this chapter, the weaponry necessary to engage confidently in spiritual warfare is presented, from a place of not only obtaining the armor, but a heart posture of following the Lord's ways in battle.

1. Shield of faith and the sword of the Spirit. Most churched people are familiar with the armor of God described in Ephesians 6:10–17. In these verses, Paul introduces important armor, but only two pieces described are not on the body of the solider; the shield of faith is one of them. The language Paul uses to describe this particular shield is very different from our typical understanding of what a shield is today.

This shield's shape was not small and circular, but instead, rectangular and the size of a door! Soldiers in Paul's day would place this shield on the ground and hide behind it, as it could cover the majority of their body and protect all other pieces of their armor. It was the first line of defense against the worst kind of weaponry: fiery darts that quickly inflicted pain and destruction.

When Paul uses this language, he connects the purpose of that door-like shield to our faith. In warfare, our faith in our constant, unchanging God is the full body armor necessary in battle. It should cover us from head to toe and be the shield that we hide behind from whatever fiery darts the enemy throws our way. We don't even have to maneuver to cover where the attack is targeted. Our faith is all-encompassing and covers anything vulnerable to assault.

Similarly, the sword of the Spirit Paul mentions is the second piece of armor not worn by a soldier. This sword would have looked like the typical Roman sword in battle—easy to pull in combat and short in length, thus making it a quick-to-use weapon in battle. In warfare, we need an easy-to-draw weapon that cuts to the core of our enemy. On a playground, a child can tell a bully what is true, and the bully can still (and often does) attack. That situation looks different, though, if the child's parent is present to speak that truth to the bully. The parent's words carry authority and protection.

If the sword of the Spirit is the spoken word of God, then we wield the very nature of God in Spirit-led words to counter our enemy. The word of God—both the *logos* and the *rhema*—is an all-encompassing weapon that covers the entire landscape of the battle and the specific combat in the moment.[7] Likewise, our shield of faith functions as the very presence of God in the battle. Countless Scriptures describe God as our shield (Prov. 30:5; Ps. 3:3; Deut. 33:29), and our faith in him is ultimately our best covering in combat.

2. The name of Jesus. In order to wield his name with victory, we must answer the question, "Do we really believe there is power in his name?" In Scripture, we have forgiveness of sin through his name and life in his name (Acts 2:38; 10:43; John 20:31). We are told that if we ask anything in his name, then he will do it (John 14:14), and that "whatever you do, in word or deed, do everything in the name of the Lord Jesus" (Col. 3:17, ESV).

> God invites us to call upon his name
> in all circumstances.

In Acts 4:12, we read that there is "no other name . . . by which we must we saved." That salvation is layered and complete—we are saved, healed, and delivered by his name. His name allows us to cast out the demonic (Mark 16:17–18), and his very name is a refuge, "The name of the LORD is a strong tower; the righteous man runs into it and is safe" (Prov. 18:10, ESV). The weapon of his name for those who believe carries the most authority and weight.

In spiritual warfare, we cannot depend on the strength of our names. We will quickly be defeated. But *his* name is already victorious and above any enemy that we will encounter: "Some trust in chariots, and some in horses; but we will remember the name of the LORD our God" (Ps. 20:7–8, NKJV).

3. Praise, worship, and intercession. When the people of God marched around the walls of Jericho, it was resounding praise that knocked the city's walls down. Imagine praise so intentionally directed to God in warfare that it evoked the response of God (Josh. 6:20).

A prison was shaken, and chains fell off in Acts 16 when Paul and Silas began to sing praises to God. In 2 Chronicles 20, Jehoshaphat appointed a choir to lead the charge against their enemies, and as they went out praising God, the Lord set ambushes against Ammon, Moab, and Mount Seir. This choir's specialty was worship, and they knew the intricacies of praise as precisely as an archer knows his bow and arrow. As a result, the enemies were ambushed and destroyed one another as well.

Is it possible that we lose many battles, not only because we neglect that secret place of worship and prayer, but also because we don't even consider worship and prayer in our strategy in warfare? The combination of worship and prayer, according to these verses, invites God's power to do the impossible. It changes our heart in the battle and is a formidable weapon against the enemy.

The last place the devil wants to reside is near the praises of God's people; he will often flee quickly when praise and worship rise in the middle of a struggle—as if he can't stand to hear it. Praise and worship combine to provoke the mightiest weapon in God himself, just like a key that unlocks a holy arsenal.

4. Rest. From the earliest pages of Scripture, God demonstrates to us the necessity of rest. He did this first by observing a Sabbath on the seventh day of creation (Gen. 2:2). Jesus tells us in Mark 2:27, "The Sabbath was made for man" and not the other way around. These two verses demonstrate how God values physical rest and that rest is good for us. Rest was made for us, as I mentioned in Chapter 4.

So why is rest necessary for battle? Many weapons we have examined up to this point require our interaction with God. Yet it is impossible for us to develop that relationship right in the middle of a spiritual air strike. We are invited into this Sabbath rest intentionally. A weary soldier is not an effective soldier, and if God demonstrates that rest is good for us, then we are foolish to run off to battle equipped with the equivalent of a spiritual nap when we needed a full night's rest. That plan just doesn't work. In battle, God is neither tired, nor rushed, nor anxious, nor stressed.

> God enters battle from a place
> of confident rest.

We are reminded again and again in Scripture to "wait for the LORD" (Ps. 27:14). We are the ones who prematurely act from a place of worry or hurriedness. Against his enemies, the Lord "laughs at the wicked, for he knows their day is coming" (Ps. 37:13). We tend to not be found laughing in battle; if anything, we are often crying and screaming.

But in the place of confident rest, the Lord laughs. He never fears missing the victory because he knows the very day and hour that the victory will be accomplished. "With God we shall do valiantly; it is he who will tread down our foes" (Ps. 60:12, ESV). Resting in him and in his ability to fight for us is a necessary weapon for warfare, and one we must sharpen as we strive to enter his rest from a place of wholehearted obedience (Heb. 4:11).

> *The last place the devil wants to reside is near the praises of God's people.*

5. Submit, resist, and draw near. James 4:7–8 contains three essential moves toward proximity to God in warfare: "Submit yourselves therefore to God. Resist the devil, and he will flee from you. Draw near to God, and he will draw near to you" (ESV). First, in the heat of the battle, we have to acknowledge that we cannot be victorious on our own. We are not strong enough, skilled enough, or powerful enough to battle a very real enemy with very real power. But God is. James's instruction here to submit means we simply acknowledge that we are in over our head and need help. *We submit* to his authority over ours and recognize quickly that he is our only hope. Submission in battle can sound a lot like, "Oh God, please help me!" because we know he is the only one who can defeat the enemy.

From that place of coming under the safety of his refuge, *we resist* the devil, which is the second move of James 4:7–8. The order here is very important, and it cannot be reversed. We must come under God in order to resist the devil. It is nearly impossible to resist the devil on our own strength. Maybe once or twice, but eventually we fail in our own pride and deception. When we submit to God, resisting is easier because we are found in God, not isolated in our own strength. We are no longer alone or championing our own cleverness in battle; instead, we have rushed to the stronghold of God for safety and strategy.

And in rushing to his stronghold, *we draw near*, which is the third move toward proximity with God. God offers us a profound weapon in proximity, which is anchored in his promise to draw near to us when we draw near to him. We are victorious in the safety of his covering, under the armor of the shadow of his wings. No weapon formed against us can prosper there.

6. Discernment. The weapon of discernment can be simply defined as:

> The ability to make discriminating judgments, to distinguish between, and recognize the moral implication of different situations and courses

> of action. It is learning to think God's thoughts after him, practically and spiritually; having a sense of God's eyes and seeing them in some measure uncovered and laid bare.[8]

In battle, this is the ability not only to recognize the spirit driving the conflict but also not to engage it with the same spirit. Recall how Elijah in 1 Kings 18 didn't get loud and dramatic when the prophets of Baal did; he fought in a completely different manner. We cannot fight fear with fear or hatred with hatred. A controlling or manipulative spirit in a person that is driving a conflict cannot be subdued with the same spirit.

Consider Luke 9:55 when the disciples wanted to call down fire on the Samaritans. Jesus rebuked them: "You do not know what manner of spirit you are of" (NKJV). We must know what spirit we are operating in before we can discern its presence in others. To grow in discernment, we must start with our own hearts and take inventory of what drives us and motivates us from a very honest posture. Without discernment, the body of Christ suffers—and suffers badly.

For example, how many church conflicts could easily be snuffed out by using discernment? How many times has someone, from an underlying need for acceptance, paraded their position of power and the person on the receiving end felt compelled to match them? Or raise them by a title or two? For example, the new deaconess is promoting her role, and another woman—the newly appointed director of Vacation Bible School (VBS)—kindly informs her that she didn't have time to consider serving that way because VBS is taking up all of her time. Plus, she's creating a new blog to help other moms on their spiritual journey. Match and one up.

All of a sudden, the new deaconess is no longer gleaming in her triumph. She decides to come at it from another angle, and through a gritted-teeth smile, she starts talking about her conversation with the pastor's wife that went on for hours. Oh yeah, for good measure her oldest child won the Bible drill in Sunday school last week. Lines and weapons are drawn, but these are the wrong boundaries and weapons, especially in the church. Both women are falling victim to the same spirit, and they are using passive-aggressive means to try to compete. The spirit of competition has taken over, and unfortunately those spirits are victorious in this scenario.

Ephesians 4:26–27 demonstrates how the enemy can attach to how we feel and gain ground: "Be angry and do not sin; do not let the sun go down on your anger, and give no opportunity to the devil" (ESV). In our example, those women are likely insecure and struggling with their identity. Those broken places are like a fly trap for the enemy to stick to and gain ground. As people of God we need to see and discern our own broken places that open doors for the enemy and intentionally address them. As we do so, our discernment grows and consequently, our grace for others does too as we recognize the broken places that allow for unholy motivations to take root.

On the other hand, if the women described above had chosen the humble route and acted with a spirit of quiet confidence in the reality that they both served the King, then that would have preserved unity of spirit. If they had operated in the truth that there is plenty of room at the table for everyone in the kingdom, it could have stopped the fight immediately.

A spirit of competition cannot take ground against a humble person with quiet confidence. That spirit doesn't even understand it. Recognizing the spirit "of the air," as Paul called it, is key to knowing how to combat it (Eph. 2:2). In spiritual warfare, there is a need for "sons of Issachar"—men and women who understand the times (1 Chron. 12:32). God does not see as we see, so we need his discernment to look at the hearts of people and thus gain the true heart of the matter for any person or issue at hand.

PERSONAL PRAYER

1. As you consider the spiritual warfare weapons I've outlined in this chapter, ask God to search your heart and reveal any lies concerning your ability to use these weapons. For example, you may believe that rest is not an effective weapon in battle for you. It may feel counterintuitive to your anxious nature. A lie you believe might be, "If I rest, I will be vulnerable. I'm not safe if I'm not on guard. I don't know how to let Jesus be my rest, especially in hard battles." The truth is, though, in Christ these weapons are accessible to you as a follower of Jesus.

   Go through the list of weapons in this chapter one by one and take inventory with the Lord of your ability to use each weapon. Write down the weapons you feel inadequate in using or that you don't generally access.

   _____

   _____

   _____

2. As you look at your list of weapons that feel out of reach, ask God to show you why you don't feel comfortable using the weapons on the list. Ask him to show you the belief that keeps you from using each one. Ask God the following questions as you process this:

   - "God, will you please show me what I'm believing about myself that would keep me from using this weapon?"
   - "God, will you please tell me when I learned the lie that this weapon was not accessible to me?"

- "God, do I have any beliefs about this weapon that are false and that keep me from using it or desiring to use it?" (For example, "I tried praying once in the name of Jesus, and it didn't work," or, "I don't like to worship; I get bored easily.")

Ask God to show you what is true about the weapons that seem elusive to you, and then ask him to guide you in using them effectively. Ask him what steps he can offer you to help you get comfortable using the weapons. What stands in your way of using these weapons?

_____

_____

_____

3. As you go throughout the coming week, practice using some of the weapons discussed in this chapter. If needed, set an alarm so that several times throughout the day, you can stop and wait on the Lord for his word for you, just like Elijah did from a place of intimacy with the Lord.

Spiritually and emotionally place yourself behind the shield of faith. Are you comfortable there? Do you feel safe there? Or do other securities seem more stable than trusting him? Try singing or worshiping God when you feel stressed, or try calling out the characteristics of God when you feel overwhelmed or angry. Even as small conflicts or problems arise this week, apply the proximity weapon with its "submit, resist, and draw near" moves before responding or forming a plan in your mind. Don't react until you try these steps first. Make a list of some of the weapons that you want to intentionally try this week.

_____

_____

_____

4. Finally, lean into the name of Jesus in every battle and ask for greater discernment to see with his eyes what is really at the core of anxiety, conflict, and discord. Above all, carve out time to rest in him. This can take many forms, but often, it takes the form of simply sitting alone with him without an agenda and allowing him time to "restore [your] soul" like he did for the psalmist (Ps. 23:3, ESV). You can even play instrumental music if helpful. Soon, you will find that five minutes of carved-out rest with him will turn into twenty minutes. Then you will crave that rest above all else, and it will become a joyful priority for you. As you look at your week, schedule time below (date and time) to allow God to restore your soul. Write your scheduled time below as a reminder to set time to encounter him.

_____

_____

_____

COMMUNITY CONNECTION

1. Share with your group the weapon that you've cultivated and that you carry well.

2. In the same manner, share a weapon that you feel inadequate using or would like to use more.

3. Then take a group inventory of all the weapons that your group army carries well. Take a look because this vision of the people of God in their strength can encourage us in times of crisis. Exhort one another in the weapons each person demonstrates, and pray that their use of these weapons increases and they sharpen their skills using them. Spend time praying for one another, speaking life into one another with regard to these strong weapons, and interceding for any places of weakness.

4. For those weapons that seem out of reach, help one another by asking the Lord why they aren't as prevalent, and then seek a holy strategy for obtaining them.

The first step in successful spiritual warfare is recognizing that you are actually in a battle. The second step is knowing that submission to God is the battle strategy all other strategies are based on. It feels counterintuitive not to fight immediately with the weapons of the world. But when we submit to God first, this allows God—who is already victorious—to fight on your behalf and simultaneously guide you in selecting his choice weapons of warfare at just the right time. He has already "rescued us from the dominion of darkness and brought us into the kingdom of the Son" (Col. 1:13). We have access to heavenly weapons from a position of secured victory.

PART 3

THE CULMINATION

Once you are connected to God and embrace the core tools for freedom in the areas that challenge you, you can experience maturity and growth. You can thrive and move toward holiness as you draw near to God from a place of freedom. In this part, you can better understand postures in prayer to help you thrive and flourish. These postures can keep the enemy from robbing your joy in challenging times. They can also set in motion a lifestyle of thriving and reaching beyond maintenance into true freedom and the abundant life of the Christian journey.

13

LAYING ASIDE BURDENS

*Let us throw off everything that hinders and the
sin that so easily entangles. And let us run with
perseverance the race marked out for us, fixing our
eyes on Jesus, the pioneer and perfector of our faith.*

— Hebrews 12:1–2

I live with a household of runners, which makes me the odd person out for sure. If I am running, then you should probably start sprinting too because something is catastrophically wrong in the universe!

My husband was a collegiate cross-country runner, and he is proudly raising our children in the sport of pushing your body to the brink of exhaustion and dehydration. I have allowed it because he keeps telling me the spiritual benefits that this sport produces. As he quotes verses like Hebrews 12:1–2, I roll my eyes. But then I cheer with tears in my eyes when my kids cross the finish line, despite their failing muscles in the blazing heat.

I cheer because their running displays something holy. Yet there is something unholy there too. It's their clothes! Dry-fit fabric, while a gift to dedicated athletes, is a nightmare for the laundry basket, and the surrounding area of the laundry basket—and honestly any room near the laundry basket. The stench of those clothes, drenched in sweat and doused in water, is enough to require professional fumigation.

In the past, my family of runners would throw off their running clothes into the laundry basket, mixing them with their daily clothes and school uniforms. My husband's running clothes would inevitably mingle with my pretty, perfume-scented clothes. The mix of sweaty running clothes with daily clothes, the cohabitation of these putrid items with the relatively clean ones, was enough to cause gagging—and the combination only amplified the foul smell.

SIN-SOAKED CLOTHES

Sin is sort of like those clothes: it may feel like one small transgression, but it has a way of mixing into every other facet of life. Like smelly running clothes placed in a laundry pile, sin has a way of merging with the other items. They begin to smell as if they too were sweaty and dirty, even if they weren't. Sin is happy to mingle and spread its smell where it can.

In my home, we now purposefully put aside the running clothes. We do not casually toss them into the abyss of the other laundry; no, we deal with them intentionally. In harsh racing conditions the clothes take on dirt, sweat, and stench. Sure, the clothes can hold those for a bit, but what would happen if my dear sweet runners did not take the clothes off and lay them aside for cleaning? Unsanitary conditions would abound and likely affect their running at some point as well.

Sin is like that. It will affect the holy race we are running if not dealt with properly. In Chapter 10 about sin and the weeds, we learned the necessary biblical business to remove sin from our garment.

> Remember, you are a holy racer
> with a holy garment.

Despite the muck of sin that may have attached itself to your clothes, it can easily be removed. While you have to deal with the sin, it's been paid for. It is not who you are. You are clean in Jesus. The victory has been won; you must embrace it and finish strong.

RUNNING WITH WEIGHT

Hebrews 12:1 sums up the sport of running so well: "Let us throw off everything that hinders and the sin that so easily entangles." Running is active and requires our engagement. It also requires a two-fold action: laying aside *both* encumbrances and sins. We must know the difference between the two. Sin is pretty easy to recognize; eventually, it has a way of making itself known, even if we've tried to deny it. We get tripped up often in a public way.

Encumbrances are a little harder to perceive. An encumbrance feels like a weight or a bulky mass—a burden that hinders the run. We feel it, our pace is slowed down by it, and the rest of our body is affected by it. This weight affects much more than just its rooted location on our bodies: it impacts our entire race. We must see it and deal with it.

If sin is the sweat on our garment that causes a stench, then these weights are a backpack of boulders that we feel compelled to sprint with. We often know they're there, but they sort of feel like ours to carry even though a skilled racer would never compete with an extra backpack of weight. The heaviness feels like a part of us, and we race as if we were meant to carry it.

If we race with Jesus, we eventually run into the invitation in Matthew 11:28–30.

> Come to me, all you who are weary and burdened, and I will give you rest. Take my yoke upon you and learn from me, for I am gentle and humble in heart, and you will find rest for your souls. For my yoke is easy and my burden is light.

The anxieties, the worry, the false responsibility of carrying a burden not meant for us to carry, and all of the what-if thoughts keep us heavy and sluggish.

THE OTHER SIDE OF THE BURDEN

Consider the heart-wrenching burden of being the oldest child of five children whose single mother is an addict. That firstborn will often take on the role of mother, father, and every other kind of caretaker to both mother and siblings. It is a hard burden to part with even into adulthood. Or the parent of a struggling teen, often taking the burden of every possible bad outcome along with the role of securing with great pain and anxiety the teen's faith, usually with destructive pressure to the already-fragile relationship.

The parent has a role, but it is quickly becoming infused with a burden that belongs to God. The parent isn't omnipotent or all-knowing but chooses to take on the responsibility that is rightly God's. Or finally, the minister who can no longer sleep at night because he is worried about the success of his church, the happiness of his flock, and every other problematic issue that has crossed his desk that day, ranging from marriages in crisis to suicidal teens to theology arguments. That is an unimaginable burden to carry.

Then on the other side of those backpacks of weight and burden, there is an invitation from Jesus to empty them and exchange them. Where sin gets cleaned off the righteous garment in the race, the backpack gets set down, and we receive something lighter that we can carry. We must throw off the burden that hinders us and receive the one he meant for us to hold. This often looks like a yoke of intercession or specific ways in which we can partner with what God is already doing. We choose not to place ourselves in authority over the situation but instead in submission to God's ways and means of working.

If I had to carry a backpack in a holy race for a long time, I would have difficulty laying it aside. It would feel personal to me and like it was a part of me. Our burdens are like that, and God knows how we are attached to them.

> *We can partner with what God is already doing.*

They often involve people and causes that we deeply love. Laying aside these burdens requires us to be intentional and careful, not thoughtless or haphazard. And they have to be put aside so we can run freely.

While we may quickly and willingly toss aside *sin* because we're convicted, *burdens* are harder to part with. We own them and protect them because those burdens matter to us. They somehow feel safer in our hands and we don't want to part with them. We unknowingly attempt to do God's job for him in carrying the heavy burden, as if he weren't qualified to handle it.

> We hoard a false responsibility of juggling God-sized weight and wonder why we are so anxious and overwhelmed.

When we continue holding those weights, they have a way of affecting how we race and distorting our identity. We walk with an elevated sense of importance the moment we take matters into our own hands. The reason we feel so miserable is that we hold things we have no business carrying.

Those burdens are often tied to our identity, and we have a hard time distinguishing what is authentically us and what doesn't belong. False humility tempts us to keep the burdens, but when we keep them, we're declaring that we know better than God and trust our own ability over his. It's subtle pride, but it's still heavy and it slowly suffocates life abundant.

Our good Father wants to heal our wounds and remove our sins, entanglements, and ungodly beliefs that block our heart from drawing near to God. But he also wants to take those burdens on himself. We cling to them because they feel like they belong to us, but a heavy burden can weigh down the child of God. He wants to take them off because he made us to run with clean garments and to run hindered no longer.

PERSONAL PRAYER

1. We know that Jesus sees all of the encumbrances and burdens that we carry. So we can go to him and simply ask, "Jesus, would you show me which burdens I am carrying around that are slowing me down?" Go to him now and write down any burdens that he brings to mind.

_____

_____

_____

_____

_____

_____

2. Choose to lay down your burdens before Jesus by praying something like,

> *Jesus, today I choose to lay down these burdens before you. I want to trade them in for the light yoke that you want me to carry. I'm sorry that I've held them so tightly and carried responsibilities that are not mine.*

After you've prayed this, record any impressions that you have as you wait on him. How do you feel trading them in? How does God respond?

_____

_____

_____

3. For each burden you lay down, ask Jesus what the lighter "burden" or yoke feels like to carry. How is it different from what you carried before? Clearly list what his burden is and what your lighter one is now that you've exchanged them and allowed him to give you the weight meant for you. Ask him to remind you of this exchange and help you not to be encumbered by those heavy weights anymore.

_____

_____

_____

_____

_____

COMMUNITY CONNECTION

1. Talk about some of the burdens you currently carry. Are there any surprises in the list that you made in question one in the Personal Prayer section when you asked the Lord to help you name them?

2. Was it difficult to set the burdens aside? Why?

3. What did taking on the light burden feel like for you? How could you tell the difference between the heavy and light burdens?

4. What is the difference between carrying a sin and carrying a burden? Can you share examples of what the two look like in your life? Do you ever see the two mixed together in your life? Can you give a specific example in your life where you carried both at the same time?

Run to the Father today with your backpack of burdens that slow you down. He is truly your only hope for lasting endurance. Run with perseverance and fix your eyes on him in every aspect of the race: to coach you, to identify your burdens, and yes, to launder the sin that threatens to stain your garment. His role of cleaning your laundry and trading in dirty garments for something beautiful should propel you back into the race with joy and thanksgiving. His heart to see you running without constraint from those old weighty backpacks is grace-filled. He not only wants you to finish the race, but to finish it well. His yoke is easy and his burden is light.

14

CASTING CROWNS

They cast their crowns before the throne, saying,
"Worthy are you, our Lord and God, to receive glory
and honor and power, for you created all things,
and by your will they existed and were created."

— Revelation 4:10–11, ESV

White clothes should be outlawed for anyone under the age of eighteen, because no matter what I try, I cannot preserve their original, pristine white color. I've actually stopped buying school uniform shirts that are white because I simply cannot take the emotional stress of keeping them white. Even if I carefully scrub off every last bit of syrup from my children's hands at breakfast, hidden spots remain. The spot goes from grimy hands to a newly washed, white shirt, and the school day begins with partially dirty clothes. That's the beginning of the day—don't even get me started on what those shirts look like when my kids arrive home in the afternoon!

TAINTED TREASURES

Similarly, a new pair of pearly white socks can immediately turn to *off-white*—or whitish gray, or brownish white. This happens when my children strut around the driveway in their white socks while practicing basketball before school, for example, oblivious to the sock damage they are causing. They don't even think about putting on shoes as they take a couple of laps on the dirty driveway in their socks. They wait to put their shoes on until right before we get in the car to leave the house. It's amazing how the purest things can become grimy.

We have long taught our children that when they get to heaven and are asked why they deserve to have access, their only answer will be "Jesus." We don't know quite how access will work, but we like to be prepared! Jesus is the Sunday school answer for sure, but at the judgment seat, the only correct answer will be his name. Our "best days" résumé is always lacking even if it reads stellar. Because no matter how good some of our accomplishments may look, even if God himself energized those accomplishments, our answer will still be Jesus.

> We cannot hold a candle, even with the most radiant crown, to the One arrayed in splendor.

Our shiniest accolades are still tainted because they're in our grip. The shine of our crowns due to promotions, positions, or giftings becomes tarnished, even if we have the purest of hearts. The crowns placed on our heads, even if by holy hands, can also become idolatrous to us the moment we catch our glimpse in the mirror. Even the most mature followers of Jesus are not immune to pride or selfishness due to their crown. We can forget too quickly who placed it there and wear it as if we own the rights to it—as if we earned it.

GOOD AND BAD CROWNS

Crowns carry a special meaning and importance in the Bible. Consider the five types of crowns in the New Testament: There is the "crown of righteousness" in 2 Timothy 4:8 for those who love and anticipate the Second Coming of Christ; the "crown of glory" in 1 Peter 5:4 for those who shepherd the flock well; the "imperishable crown" in 1 Corinthians 9:25 for those who practice self-denial and self-control in the Christian race; the "crown of life" (ESV) in Revelation 2:10 for those who persevere under trials; and the "crown of rejoicing" (NKJV) in 1 Thessalonians 2:19 for those who spread the gospel.

Theologians differ on whether these are five separate crowns or one crown that encompasses all of these descriptions. Whatever the case, a holy crown is prized among believers, and when we receive one, we should be quick to cast it off in the presence of the most beautiful Jesus, as demonstrated by the elders in Revelation 4.

The elders around God's throne in Revelation 4 model for us the right posture to take with regard to our crowns. John writes, "They cast their crowns before the throne" (Rev. 4:10, ESV). The Greek word for "cast" here (ballōœ) means "to throw off" or "to let go" of a thing without caring where it falls.[9] What makes this word unique is the "without caring where it falls" part. I don't know about you, but if I had a crown, I wouldn't want to take it off in the first place! And I most certainly would care about where it fell. Have you ever seen a little girl with a princess crown? Prying that crown out of her grimy princess hands wouldn't be easy if you tried! Like her, we all like to hold on to our treasures.

Historically, crown-casting demonstrated a significant power play in war. For example, Tigranes, the king of Armenia, cast his crown before Pompey after being captured by the Roman general. Pompey had the power to treat Tigranes in any way he desired, but Pompey raised the king up and put the crown back on his captive's head. Similarly, Herod removed his own crown after meeting Caesar. After Herod spoke pleasing words to Caesar, Caesar placed Herod's crown back on him.[10]

Kings casting their crowns to other kings is an inspiring thought. Yet the kings received their crowns back upon their heads. The ones who placed the crown back on their heads did so with dirty motives and tricky power plays, because remember these were pagan leaders, renegades, and scoundrels. Manipulation and a good dose of flattery motivated the politics of the time.

But in the Revelation throne room, saints who were once sinners throw off crowns that were bestowed by their Beloved, without a care of getting them back or even where they land. Their crown-throwing disavows any independence they might have or ownership over their treasured crown. It demonstrates the highest respect and homage for the One whom they worship. In their position they choose humility, and even with the gifts of crowns, they remain submissive and cast the crowns, with all honor and glory given to the One who deserves it all. How radiant he must have been—and remains today—that the elders would quickly toss their crowns without a care as to where they land! God gives us a crown for our reward, and we give our reward right back to him.

> *Saints who were once sinners throw off crowns that were bestowed by their Beloved.*

CASTING OUR CROWNS

I've made a habit of taking the crowns I have been given and casting them back to the Lord. It is a safety net for me—to hand them over quickly in prayer. When I hold them too tightly, the crowns become a source of anxiety and a burden I can't properly carry. When I begin to feel as though I've earned those crowns, I toss them fast—as if they were fire that would burn my head or hands to keep them longer. There is danger in spending too much time admiring the crowns instead of the Giver of them.

> The crowns must return to the One
> who deserves them all.

The elders in the throne room were giving up good crowns given by Jesus. Those biblical crowns were gifts, and in his presence, they didn't need them or want them. They looked at him and decided he was worth it all. We want those crowns and a life that secures them. But there are unholy crowns that we pine after much more on this side of eternity: unholy crowns like platforming for position or competing for success. The truth is, there is often a reward there, produced by bad motivation or subtle manipulation. It is a worldly crown that offers instant gratification for a need to be important, but that crown tarnishes quickly. People see it, but it never truly satisfies.

Consider the young man who in his youth decided that he was called to ministry. He began to call himself a preacher and declared he was put on earth to do this. The role of preacher became his crown. When his vocation didn't look exactly like he expected, however, he became disillusioned and wandered from distraction to distraction in ministry. The role and title, the crown, became his identity, and he was stuck there. He couldn't take it off because his worth was so tied to it. It was a premature crown forced into his hands that never fulfilled him. As a result, he considered departing from ministry altogether and only stuck it out half-heartedly. On most days he questioned the goodness of God and grew in disappointment.

Our quick-fix culture holds crowns tightly because we haven't taken first steps in our identity with God. Think about the many people who believe they are meant to do something "big" or be someone "famous." They might have a good crown given by God, but it's never enough. The cubic zirconia crown that the world teases seems much more valuable than the real one they have. They miss what God has given and will do anything to hold the counterfeit crown. And they walk disappointed and ineffective in their spiritual life. The respect of others can start as a good crown that can quickly tarnish if it defines us and fuels our worth. Many of us have a collection of unholy crowns that has not given us the recognition we crave.

The solution is the same with both kinds of crowns. If I don't give the crowns up daily, they can quickly define my identity and likely distort it. But when I cast them one by one, I can, with full thanksgiving, be grateful they've been returned back to Jesus, who really does deserve ownership of every single one. And as I do, I take stock of my worth with and without the crowns. Am I worthy if I don't put the crowns back on? Does my worth change if I do?

The truth is, my worth has already been secured and stays the same no matter what. Casting the crowns is a shift in focus back to the Savior, who is more precious than any jeweled ornament on my head—more treasured than any promotion, accolade, gift, or position. If the crown becomes what holds my gaze, then I am not gazing where I should. I look to Jesus and give the crown back.

PERSONAL PRAYER

1. Ask the Father to show you if there are any crowns you wear that aren't biblical crowns. In light of anticipating Jesus' return, shepherding people well, showing self-denial in the race of faith, persevering under trials, and sharing the gospel—all holy biblical crowns—many of our worldly accolades and accomplishments won't hold up in comparison. They will all burn up, but biblical crowns live on. We must deal with the unholy crowns that feel true. They may appear as good things, such as leadership positions, ministry progress, or accolades in work, but they can become distorted and carry too much importance in our lives. Ask the Father to help you name your unholy crowns, which give you a counterfeit identity or feel important but will perish next to the holy, biblical ones.

_____

_____

_____

2. Once you name the unholy crowns, cast them away from you. Ask for help here if you need it because it's sometimes hard to lay down what has defined us. As you throw off any unholy crowns (even crowns that started out holy but are now tarnished), pay attention to Jesus' response. Use all of your senses to do this. Listen, look, and sense his response as you cast away those crowns. As you do this, record any impressions that you have about how Jesus responds to your casting of these false crowns.

_____

_____

_____

3. Ask the Lord to show you any crown that has been bestowed by him. These are the good crowns—the ones that really matter. Then cast these crowns back to him. These crowns are areas where his favor and his gifting are evident. Where his Spirit enables you to persevere or have abundant faith or deny yourself. Pay attention to your heart as you cast these good crowns back to God, and look to Jesus for his response. List the good crowns and the truth that God gives about them.

_____

_____

_____

4. In light of the reality of biblical crowns to come (2 Tim. 4:8; 1 Peter 5:4; 1 Cor. 9:25; Rev. 2:10; 1 Thess. 2:19), ask Jesus to help you desire those crowns above all else. Think about them and focus your attention on how much they matter. Ask God if anything stands in your way of desiring those eternal rewards. Write down the things that might hinder those rewards.

_____

_____

_____

5. In heaven, there will be no jealousy or disappointment. We all will be fully satisfied in the Lord. But we will be rewarded for what we do here. That is, what we do here will determine what we do in eternity. Eternity will welcome all followers of Jesus, but for those who stored up their treasures in heaven, rewards will follow based on their decisions in this life (Matt. 6:19–21).

Ask the Lord to show you the rewards he wants you to pursue. Ask for greater desire for and the ability to pursue these lasting rewards. Write a prayer that displays your conviction, your desire for the eternal reward, and any other responses that surface. It could be as simple as, "Lord, I want to choose the rewards that align to your truth. I am asking for a greater desire to pursue those crowns."

_____

_____

_____

COMMUNITY CONNECTION

1. As a group, share with one another some of the unholy crowns and holy crowns that you carry.

2. What is harder to cast aside for you: the unholy crowns or the ones that matter?

3. How can you position your heart to see the coming rewards as more important than the fleeting ones of this life?

4. What happens when you as a group fix your eyes on Jesus—his radiance, his power, and his mercy—and corporately cast your crowns, listing them together and declaring they are cast? Fix your eyes on Jesus and cast your crowns before him as a group, aloud and one at a time. Just like a worship chorus sung by many voices swells the heart, a group who casts their crowns is a powerful depiction of what is to come. Doing so is an act of sacrificial worship and positions us where we need to be—with our eyes on Jesus and our crowns cast.

> Commit this week to make a practice of casting crowns before God. They belong to him. We did not earn them, so he can have them all. Whatever holy things God has bestowed, give them back willingly—he is worthy of every crown, every kingdom, and every honor. "Worthy are you, our Lord and God, to receive glory and honor and power, for you created all things, and by your will they existed and were created" (Rev. 4:11, ESV).

15

HOLDING HOLY AUTHORITY

For whoever exalts himself will be humbled, and
he who humbles himself will be exalted.
— Luke 14:11, NASB

A few years ago, I did intensive physical therapy to try and save my very diseased right knee, which was dying a slow death, like the left knee before it had due to a disease called necrosis (a rare diagnosis). Day after day, painful hour after hour, I did everything imaginable with the best orthopedic technology to build back my knee, but it was beyond repair. If a knee could have a rehabilitative support team around it, this orthopedic center was the place to get it. Yet despite all of my extensive personal effort—combined with a team of amazing specialists—no one could save my knee from dying.

Before we came to this realization, though, one afternoon at the conclusion of my therapy, I was flat on my back with my right knee high in the air. The majority of my leg was swallowed in an ice machine, which kept my knee elevated. The machine pulsed with cold water around my knee. I watched the machine contract and expand, the water inside it moving back and forth. Then I closed my eyes, both in a response to the rhythm and in an attempt to keep my peace.

Moments later, I heard the voice of the woman in charge of the facility telling the therapists and technicians who I was and what I did. For some strange reason she was on the rehab floor that day. She spoke not about my dying knee, but about ministry and calling. She knew me from church and had heard me speak about Freedom Prayer. I was inwardly struggling with the harsh reality of a looming second knee replacement in my thirties, yet she spoke to the room about my purpose in life. I was drowning in grief about what was before me, and she was calling me up in the middle of it all. I felt my face blush in contrast to my very cold leg.

In that moment, the truth of how God works in raising people up into greater authority came flooding into my heart. It was as if he instantly spoke, "This is how I do things: You are completely flat on your back, laid up, and limping. You could not elevate yourself even if you wanted to—physically or spiritually. You can't even get up. But you don't need to. I will call you up." It wasn't audible, but I heard his voice loud and clear.

JESUS' EXAMPLE AND HOLY AUTHORITY

Having to endure the process of physical recovery and healing is so humbling because during it we need assistance with the most basic tasks. We can't do anything alone. But in those quiet and hidden moments, we can learn about holy authority. Holy authority is dependent on the timing and power of God for anointed position and purpose. In essence, it looks like Jesus obediently responding to the will of the Father, full of the Spirit, in total submission to his ways and his plan.

Holy authority is the opposite of the world's authority, which *demands* position and power. It does what no one sees coming. When the world expects posturing, holy authority steps back, waits, and goes low. Worldly authority bulldozes for the purpose of self-promotion and self-preservation, while holy authority preserves others, sometimes even requiring great personal sacrifice and risk.

When we contemplate holy authority, we must start with Jesus, who so boldly proclaimed that all authority in heaven and on earth had been given to him (Matt. 28:18). He did not manipulate his way into holding supremacy; he received it. The crowds noticed his authority, for Jesus "taught as one who had authority, and not as their teachers of the law" (Matt. 7:29). Holy authority, as perfectly demonstrated by Jesus, was both given to him and acknowledged by others. Therefore, when we carry any degree of holy authority, people will recognize it because it is otherworldly. We don't need to proclaim for validation; people quickly acknowledge this kind of authority when they see it.

What was it about Jesus that allowed him to carry the gift of his holy authority? While he was God incarnate, he still navigated his personal ministry in great humility with both ears listening to the Father. He spoke only the words given by the Father. Obedience to the Father prompted everything he did. That truth alone shatters so much of what we laud as "authority" in our culture! How many deeds do we perform without even slightly engaging the Father? And how many acts do we achieve in a hurried fashion for the sake of personal gain?

> *When we carry any degree of holy authority, people will recognize it because it is otherworldly.*

Jesus did not rush toward fame and fortune in his young twenties like so many do fresh out of college. Instead, he waited until he was thirty years old to step into ministry. Even then he often preferred his holy acts to remain unseen and unspoken. He had no interest in a reputation but purposely removed himself from accolades until the time chosen by the Father to save his people. He washed feet, pardoned sinners, and healed the sick in town by town—all while investing in a few who would follow him and learn from him.

He freely gave of himself, never hoarding what he had. He did nothing showy, nothing prideful, and when people noticed, he often removed himself from the crowd to seek the Father. The intentional, small decisions he made over and over again brought transformation for the masses. He did not think "high and lofty" but acted in small ways—one small act by one small act—and that formed a harvest that reached beyond what his hands touched.

ESTHER'S EXAMPLE

We see examples in the Old Testament of this type of holy authority that Jesus modeled long before his birth and ministry. For example, Esther arrived on the scene "for such a time as this" (Est. 4:14, ESV), her life's example pointing to Jesus, who would come and save all people at just the right time.

Esther's story began as King Ahasuerus looked for a new wife after Queen Vashti disobeyed him. She was selected as her replacement from a group of hopeful queens. Later, the evil Haman sought to have all of the Jews killed, but Esther, at the prompting of her cousin and guardian Mordecai, strategically intervened. Esther's submissive actions and humility saved a people group in danger of losing their lives.

If there is a pattern that exists in individuals who carry this holy authority, Esther demonstrated a heart that was both prepared and ready to receive what was given to her. She could humbly carry both. Holy authority cannot be fabricated by an individual, but a person can be positioned to obtain it at just the right time. We can glean much from her actions and words that show her capacity to hold holy authority.

Esther's example of holy authority begs the question: *What do you lead with?* In other words, when you walk into a room, what goes before you? Are people met with an unseen pride or covert insecurity? Even the least discerning people can pick up on what someone enters a room carrying. Is it fear? Is there a perceived joy? Consider walking into a party. What comes in before you and is the first thing people sense? Is it what you do instead of who you are? Does your truest identity get shrouded under your job or gifts in ministry? Do you lead with what you hope people will see or with your authentic self?

> *Holy authority cannot be fabricated by an individual.*

From the moment Esther is introduced in the narrative, we see a quiet wisdom that portrays a heart ready to receive authority. Let me be clear: it is very true that Esther and Vashti did not have much choice culturally about obeying what they were asked to do. The men who dominated their kingdom gave offensive orders that gave women like them no option.

We can sympathize with Vashti, even if she was obstinate, that she did not want to be paraded through her husband's intoxicated party. We also sympathize with Esther, as she likely had no choice in being brought into the gathering like a reality show's parade of women. Despite these appalling realities, we cannot negate the hidden wisdom of God on display within this story.

> God has a way of bringing holiness to a mess.

Esther had holy authority and not because she jockeyed for position; she received it because she was willing to die for her people. We gain holy authority, like she did, by being willing to die to our pride, our selfish motivations, our vain hopes, our talents, and even sometimes our life. Jesus exemplified this with his own death and resurrection: "Truly, truly I say to you, unless a grain of wheat falls into the earth and dies, it remains alone; but if it dies, it bears much fruit" (John 12:24, NASB).

FIVE PRECURSORS TO HOLY AUTHORITY

We can see five precursors in Esther's story that position her heart to receive holy authority. These are postures we should emulate and desire. We should also look for ways to cultivate them, even in small decisions. Those precursors, practiced in hidden ways, set a foundation ready to receive authority from God at his anointed time. The ground that has been obediently disciplined can hold the platform given by the Father.

1. A submissive spirit. Esther was an orphan, adopted by Mordecai as his own daughter, although they were cousins. When Esther was taken into the king's palace in the court of women, she was immediately shown favor by the attendants but followed Mordecai's instructions not to make known "her nationality and family background" (Esther 2:10). Despite instant admiration by those in charge, Esther stayed true to Mordecai's advice and kept silent.

I would imagine that it didn't even cross her mind to do otherwise. If holy authority exists to preserve a people, there would likely be other key players involved, such as a Mordecai, advising and mentoring in such an important task. In our society, we often disregard wise words that don't immediately make sense or seem to fit our plan. And submission has been so badly twisted by the world (and by the church if we're honest) that it looks nothing like it should. Esther's submission to Mordecai was not demeaning, and Mordecai was not domineering. Trust and safety were in the instructions—not to mention an understanding of timeliness and protection. This is what she had always done under his care. Her heart did not learn a new lesson in this transition; instead, her heart beat true to her nature from the start, which had been cultivated before this point in time.

2. Patience. It took Esther twelve months of beautification to get ready to meet the king. This is mind-blowing because at this point in my life I can be ready in exactly twenty-five minutes for anything fancy. Her beautification lasted for months, which is absurd to me. But remember, we can still find God's holy plans at work in the midst of the absurd. We tend to want to speed up any preparation process in order to do the next thing or to move up a tier in our pursuits. Maybe it's not physical preparation, but no matter what we're waiting for, it can still be worth it. The idea of a year of getting ready might sound ridiculous to us, but what if that waiting and preparing—even if we think we are ready—is worth the position it places our hearts in?

3. Receiving counsel. When it was finally time to see the king, the women in the king's court were allowed to take anything from their quarters to the king's palace that they desired. When it was Esther's turn, she "did not request anything except what Hegai, the king's eunuch who was in charge of the women, advised" (Esther 2:15, NASB). The conclusion of that verse reads, "And Esther was finding favor in the eyes of all who saw her."

> *We can still find God's holy plans at work in the midst of the absurd.*

Yes, this year-long beautification process was archaic and makes us squirm today, but this woman is responsible for Purim—an entire Jewish holiday commemorating the saving of the Jewish people. She sought advice and found favor in the middle of the waiting process. Her actions demand our close eye. She simply sought counsel with the one who oversaw her. She took only what the king's eunuch suggested. She could have taken anything and everything but asked for wisdom. Again, she had a heart positioned for holy authority.

4. Developing a strategy. We are not talking at all about a business model for success here. When Esther learned that Haman had an edict for the destruction of the Jews, she instructed Mordecai and her people to fast for three days. Esther and her maidens chose the same fast.

Holy authority dictates holy strategy.

And holy strategy is often found in fasting and prayer. Again and again throughout the Scriptures, God's people sacrifice their comfort and satisfaction in order to position their hearts toward him.

5. Using discernment. Essentially, the story of Esther shows that she knew which battles to pick and how to pick them. She was the queen, yet she did not flippantly use her position or presume to use her power. She realized the law and that she could indeed die for approaching the king uninvited. Yet when he saw her in the outer court, she obtained his favor. Then in an attempt to comfort her obviously worried heart, he offered her half of the kingdom. Her discernment here was profound.

If it had been me, once the king's scepter was extended, I would have likely blurted out the fact that *his buddy Haman* was out to destroy my people. But she waited. She planned a banquet and invited the king and Haman to attend. She showed discernment about how to save her people, even at the risk of her own life. Because of her discernment, Haman's plot was foiled and he lost his life; Mordecai was promoted; the Jewish people had "happiness and joy, gladness and honor" (Est. 8:16); and Esther wrote with "full authority" (Est. 9:29) in establishing Purim.

Esther truly lived a "life worthy of the calling [she had] received" (Eph. 4:1). Not only that, but she also walked out the words of 1 Peter 2:13, submitting herself "for the Lord's sake" to the earthly and often distorted institutions that she culturally found herself in as she rescued a people. She had been given holy authority, as I mentioned, "for such a time as this" (Est. 4:14, ESV), but her heart had been earlier positioned and prepared for that appointed time.

Esther's life invites us to examine our own histories with a view on where we've been formed to receive holy authority. We often look with disdain on seasons of waiting and seeking wisdom, wishing that they would pass. But we can look with new eyes and receive waiting as the process that births patience, and submitting as that which produces wisdom. We can remember in it all the truth that humility like this can literally save a people. Esther's holy authority was fashioned long before she stepped foot in the king's court. And "for such a time" she was exalted.

PERSONAL PRAYER

1. As you consider the holy authority that Jesus possessed, and to a lesser degree that Esther displayed, read through any passages displaying the authority of Jesus (e.g., John 7:53–8:11; John 13:1–7). Pause to notice the way he demonstrated holy strategy (Luke 6:12–13; Luke 5:16) and how he intentionally used his authority (Heb. 10:7; Matt. 21:4; John 4:4–26). Write any observations that stand out to you as you read these examples.

_____

_____

_____

_____

_____

2. Ask the Lord to show you specific places where the world's definition of authority—the power or right to give orders, make decisions, and enforce obedience—has tainted the biblical sense of holy authority. Put the items of your list in the columns below to see any discrepancies—not only in how the world obtains authority, but also the measures through which the world attempts to secure it and keep it. Examples are in italics.

WORLDY AUTHORITY	HOLY AUTHORITY
Large and domineering *Self-serving*	*Like a lamb* *Selfless*

3. Allow the Lord permission to search your heart regarding the word "submission." Again, Jesus offered the ultimate display of submission in his perfect presentation of a life bent to the Father's will. And consider Esther and how she submitted without question to Mordecai who had raised her. Ask the Lord to compare the world's counterfeit display of submission and what he truly intended by that posture he expects of us. Record below any insight that he gives as you seek his truth.

_____

_____

_____

4. A good father knows his children's hearts and the specific reasons why they cannot wait or be still. Ask God, our heavenly Father, to show you the number-one reason why you hesitate to wait on him. What do you believe will be lost or missed if you wait? Also, do you believe in obtaining a holy strategy from God? Why or why not?

_____

_____

_____

5. If you struggle with "picking battles"—as in all the battles are always yours to fight—ask the Lord where that struggle comes from. What do you falsely believe about yourself that makes you pick the wrong battles? What do you falsely believe about others? Ask the Lord to reveal those lies that prompt you toward conflict.

_____

_____

_____

COMMUNITY CONNECTION

1. Which of Esther's five precursors is most difficult for you personally? Do you struggle with the concept of submission? Is it difficult to be patient? Is counsel hard for you to receive? Why?

2. Have you been adversely affected by unholy authority? In what way? What did it produce in you? Did the actions of one (or a few) taint the concept of what good authority looks like?

3. Have you ever seen a demonstration of holy authority? Who was your example of walking in holy authority? What was it about them that was different? How did you know? What did it produce?

> God's kingdom works completely opposite of the world's, especially when it comes to power and authority. If we as sons and daughters manipulate our way to position, we choose our reward and it will not be one that lasts. Holy authority is birthed in hidden submission, waiting, wise counsel, strategy, and discernment. Also, it is often found in small ways before being used for the greater good. Ask God for these precursors to holy authority to become natural for you and for greater trust in what can be birthed from them. He is ready for the people of God to walk as they should, as servant leaders moving in holy authority for the sake of his kingdom.

16

EMBRACING SUFFERING

And the God of all grace, who called you to his eternal glory
in Christ, after you have suffered a little while, will himself
restore you and make you strong, firm and steadfast.

— 1 Peter 5:10

Have you ever put off today what you hope you will forget tomorrow because you know it's going to be painful? For example, how many times have you procrastinated scheduling a dreaded dentist appointment? A dental visit can quickly remind us that not only our bodies but also our minds and hearts are frail—we find ourselves feeling helpless in that chair and brace for imminent doom, whether or not it's actually there.

I remember when I was a young mom, standing in my kitchen, listening to my husband talk about suffering after he had been studying Paul's letters. Paul spoke in depth about this topic, offering that we should "rejoice in our sufferings, knowing that suffering produces endurance" (Rom. 5:3–4, ESV), which leads to so many other good qualities. Paul knew suffering, and my worst days do not compare to some of his.

Examining Paul's life produced in my husband a perspective toward suffering that he hadn't had before. It was a perspective I certainly hadn't had either. He said he wouldn't ask for suffering necessarily, but he wouldn't run from it either, after seeing the unmistakable fruit it birthed in Paul's relationship with God. I shushed him because the thought of suffering horrified me. We had little babies, and I could not imagine willingly adding suffering to the picture.

In the years that followed, we experienced our own measures of suffering—some light and momentary afflictions. Others became trials that lasted years. One for me was the mysterious bone disease that took my knees that I mentioned in the previous chapter. It was a nine-year struggle that introduced me to what has been called "the dark night of the soul."

> In that pit: I learned to depend on
> Jesus completely . . .

. . . not only for my peace, but for my provision and the ability to literally take the next step. It pressed me to my core, but there was gold on the other side.

In the middle of both big and small suffering, my husband and I clung to the promises of a good God even when those promises seemed to be a very dim light in a very dark place. I held on to the truths of God's ways, even when those truths seemed to slip through my fingers. And as much as I wanted the suffering to end, when I look back now, I would not trade it for anything. I could not have gained what I did without suffering. The suffering produced something that my relatively easy life could not. No matter how badly I wanted my pain to end as I endured it, I am who I am because of my suffering.

THE PRODUCT OF PAIN

So how do Christians respond in prayer when suffering hits? How do we find the goodness of God in the middle of excruciating pain? How do we reconcile his allowing suffering to take place and his being a good Father?

Omitting suffering in our journey toward freedom in Christ would be a disservice not only to God and his holiness but also to our sanctification—the process of becoming more like Jesus. We would like to omit suffering, but we can't. It's inevitable. The Scriptures tell us we will suffer (John 16:33; 2 Cor. 4:17; 2 Tim. 3:12). But we are in good company—God did not remove suffering from his own Son.

The span that we will suffer varies, as does its impact on each individual. The measure of suffering looks different from person to person, even when facing identical hardships. Still, suffering often knocks the air out of our faith faster than anything else. Even amid suffering that drops like a bomb in the middle of the night, we must cling to demonstrations of God's heart and truth found in Scripture. We know that at an ordained time God will restore what the suffering stole.

In 1 Peter 5:10, the apostle Peter reminds us of this truth: "And the God of all grace, who called you to his eternal glory in Christ, after you have suffered a little while, will himself restore you and make you strong, firm and steadfast." These verses remind us of the same truth:

> Our light and momentary troubles are achieving for us an eternal glory that far outweighs them all. (2 Cor. 4:17)
>
> It was good for me to be afflicted so that I might learn your decrees. (Ps. 119:71)
>
> Blessed is the one who perseveres under trial because, having stood the test, that person will receive the crown of life that the Lord has promised to those who love him. (James 1:12)
>
> I have told you these things, so that in me you may have peace. In this world you will have trouble. But take heart! I have overcome the world. (John 16:33)
>
> I want you to know Christ—yes, to know the power of his resurrection and participation in his sufferings, becoming like him in his death. (Phil. 3:10)

These Scriptures point to something gained on the other side of suffering, with the utmost gain our becoming like Jesus. Compared to God's restoration, no matter how bad the suffering, it is quick and light in comparison to the restoration that awaits us. That's not to say that God diminishes the pain or the severity of our suffering. Remember, Jesus is familiar with any pain we bear, but what he gives us in return makes any agony we might experience fade away.

Consider a time when you didn't have anything to eat all day long. You were tired, hungry, and likely in a foul mood. In your flesh, all you could think about was when you could eat and how your stomach growled. Your focus was on the solution to your hunger. But when you ate again, you forgot how your body reacted to hunger, because you were satisfied by the goodness of the food. You were thankful and filled. Restoration after suffering is like that. You remember the bad but rejoice in the good. And the good has a way of doing away with the bad.

OUR SAVIOR AND OUR SUFFERING

The suffering I see around me often overwhelms me. I struggle to watch the news. I don't know if I can take hearing of another tragedy or blatant act of evil executed on the innocent. I have sat and wept with far too many people whose lives were turned upside down. I have heard things that I cannot unhear and that carry an unspeakable depravity and anguish. I have experienced suffering I didn't see coming and watched it attempt to rob every bit of joy I had.

Yet no matter how awful our suffering, we can look to Jesus, who on the cross endured the weight of suffering and sin heaped upon his shoulders. Imagine Jesus taking upon himself all our suffering: every abuse, every sickness, every manipulation, every war, every hatred, every unimaginable painful heartache that ever took place. Jesus hung on the cross with all of that suffering pounding down on him during his most painful moment.

Because of what he accomplished on the cross, however, he now holds the keys to the restoration for which we cry out. When suffering tests our faith, we can take comfort in the words of Jesus, who uttered the distressed cry, "My God, my God, why have you forsaken me?" (Matt. 27:46). Thus, Jesus fully understands how suffering can make us question everything, even the goodness of the Father.

If we are comforted by the suffering of Jesus, we must also cling to the outcome of his suffering. The cross was the opening scene of Jesus' restoration story. After his resurrection and ascension, he returned to the right hand of God, where he intercedes for us and allows us to be seated with him (Eph. 2:6).

> *The cross was the opening scene of Jesus' restoration story.*

This means we now have access to something above the suffering that threatens to pull us under. We have access to the One who literally went to the depths of hell and now sits higher than all of the suffering and pain.

Allow the magnitude of that truth to settle in: even in our darkest nights of the soul, we are seated with Jesus, the One who knows and responds to our pain. His suffering, like ours, was not wasted. It produced something in him no one else could: his ascension and endowment with authority that loudly declare the truth of a promised restoration to the world.

What if our suffering is intended to offer restoration for the world as well? How many times have we watched someone walk through the unimaginable and our faith was strengthened because of what we learned from them? Could part of the redemption process be that God uses you to strengthen others when they face suffering?

> Jesus' suffering benefitted the masses, and our suffering can benefit others too.

We take comfort in the truth that Jesus suffered and that he intercedes for us in our own anguish (Heb. 7:25). He is well-acquainted with grief and invites us to draw near to him. In the middle of bone-crushing suffering, we are invited to come close to him. Where Jesus felt the absence of the Father on the cross, his ascension became for him—and secured for us—nearness to the Father.

We can come boldly to the throne of his grace to find help in time of need because Jesus makes that possible (Heb. 4:16). And his example reminds us what our suffering will produce if we cling to him—restoration that far outweighs any affliction we might face. We must anchor our hope to him. He wants us near; his heart beats to work out all things for good. All of it.

If we consider the scene that day on Calvary, I imagine the demons howling, perched and ready to claim victory. I can see the grief of those who loved Jesus, the confusion and fear settling in like the dark clouds that covered the sky. And in the midst of that grief was the holy Father, who was not surprised by any of it. He knew he needed to respond with finality to the sins of the world. And his heart broke watching his Son suffer.

Part of walking through suffering well is not losing sight of the Father's heart in it all. We can withstand a lot if we know who he is and how he responds to us. We can persevere if we know he is near. I take tremendous comfort in how Jesus handled his suffering. Also when I see how Paul, along with the other apostles and saints in the Bible, handled suffering, I too can, even with shaky hands, recognize that suffering produces fruit that a comfortable life cannot.

OUR SEAT AT THE TABLE

When my worst fears of suffering seem looming and imminent, I am reminded of God's heart in the story of Mephibosheth. According to 2 Samuel 4, Mephibosheth was five years old when he lost his father, Jonathan, and grandfather, King Saul, in battle. Upon the news of the deaths, Mephibosheth's nurse fled with him in a panic. But in her hurried state, he fell from her grasp. As a result, he became unable to walk. We don't hear about Mephibosheth again until later in his life, but imagine the trauma of those years in between. That kind of wartime fleeing likely remained etched on his heart and mind, along with the daily reminder of his inability to walk. He was young and innocent; he didn't deserve that kind of pain.

> *We can persevere if we know he is near.*

Years later, King David sought to show someone from "the house of Saul" kindness for the sake of his deceased friend Jonathan (2 Sam. 9:1). A servant, Ziba, told David that there was still a son of Jonathan who was alive but crippled in both feet. David called Mephibosheth to him, and Mephibosheth arrived likely fearing for his life as he managed to prostrate himself before the king. David responded, "Do not fear, for I will show you kindness for the sake of your father Jonathan, and I will restore to you all the land of Saul your father, and you shall eat at my table always" (2 Sam. 9:7, ESV).

We see God's perfect heart displayed in this imperfect king. The kindness of God toward us in our suffering is immeasurable. David's covenant promise to Jonathan compelled him to restore Mephibosheth completely in any way that he could. Can you imagine the scene in David's throne room? Mephibosheth fearing for his life, and David, relieved that he had found a member of Saul's household to bless, even though grieving at the sight of this broken man. In his kindness David made two important declarations:

- All of the land that belonged to Mephibosheth's family would be restored.
- Mephibosheth would always eat at the king's table.

In a moment, the land was completely restored. Not only that, but also Mephibosheth sat at the table with King David like a royal son. That's restoration and then some! David added to the riches when he declared that servants would cultivate the land and bring the produce for Mephibosheth to eat. If David's actions were representative of the heart of God, then we see how this restoration more than made up for what was lost.

Yet 2 Samuel 9 ends with a reminder that even in his restoration, Mephibosheth was still lame (v. 13). Sometimes on this side of eternity, accidents happen, wars rage on, and people have lasting reminders of tragedy. Mephibosheth remained lame, but he sat as a king's son at the table.

God's heart about suffering is the same today. We may walk with reminders and loss, but his response to our suffering is to invite us to his table and restore us. In his kingdom economy, pain is met with a king on a throne who wipes every tear, if not now, then soon (Rev. 21:4). What we cannot provide for ourselves, he offers in kindness and mercy.

Even with lame feet that never healed, Mephibosheth's love for his king overrode any need or bitterness that he felt. Later, Ziba lied to David about Mephibosheth's loyalty after Absalom led a rebellion, saying that he was waiting to be restored. As a result, David took everything away from Mephibosheth (2 Sam. 16). But despite losing everything once again, all Mephibosheth wanted was his king to come home safely after David had to flee. Mephibosheth didn't wash his clothes or trim his moustache after David left; he was laser-focused on the return of David. The nearness of David was everything to him (2 Sam. 19).

NEARNESS TO GOD

During our suffering, the nearness of God is everything to us. What if we counted everything loss just to look upon our King? To see him at the table and know that he has our best interests in mind no matter what. That his heart is to give back the land, to have us eat with him, and to provide for us in ways that we cannot provide for ourselves. That kind of invitation from the Lord is so profoundly good that even consistent suffering does not bother us as much as the apparent absence of our Lord.

When we suffer, we're often tempted by the enemy to believe two lies:

- God is not near.
- God is not good.

This story shows the opposite of these lies: God invites us to come close to him in our pain. He remembers his promises. He restores what was lost. He is good. Mephibosheth was unkempt because he simply wanted his master back at the table. He didn't care about the second loss of inheritance. He just wanted to be near his king.

At the height of my pain during my nine years of suffering, I remember the day when I stopped crying out for some sort of resolution before God, and instead cried, "I just need you to be near." Then a peace that truly passed my own understanding settled deep in me, and I knew that as long as he was near to me, whatever happened would be okay. Like Mephibosheth, I could not stand, could not walk, and could not focus on anything else through mind-numbing pain—unless he was near. That kind of suffering was not wasted because of what it produced in me. It killed my knees, but it also killed my self-sufficiency and my perceived ability to navigate life in my own strength.

At the end of that suffering was abiding. His nearness was all I craved. I didn't have to seek it or search for it anymore. Suffering had removed every hindrance, and I found him to be always near. And it was worth it. When we pass through grief, pain, and loss and have nothing left, God becomes everything. And once we know him as everything, he truly takes his rightful place in our heart. Before suffering, I knew a Christian life of still walking in my own abilities. After suffering, I lean only on my Beloved.

PERSONAL PRAYER

1. Often in suffering, we can recall what is true biblically in our mind, but our heart cries out for more—for answers. We feel torn in it all and split in our convictions. But God knows our heart better than we do, and he knows our struggles too. As you consider periods of suffering in your own life, did you ever believe the lie that God wasn't good or that he wasn't near? Did your suffering attempt to snuff out your longstanding faith? Ask the Lord to show you if those lies were present in your seasons of suffering and if there was one that felt stronger. Write what lies felt stronger in those seasons and what they produced.

_____

_____

_____

_____

_____

2. Would you trade in suffering for an easy life if you knew that also meant not being close to God? Really allow yourself time to sit with this question. Suffering has a way of sifting our motives and convictions. Write down your prayer to God as you share your truest response to this question.

_____

_____

_____

3. Mephibosheth's suffering and restoration produced in him a deep love for King David. Focus especially on what suffering might have internally produced in you. Is it a steadiness in times of trial? Is it a humility that you didn't have before? Ask the Lord to show you the good that came in your suffering.

_____

_____

_____

4. In contrast, what do you feel *the enemy* has tried to produce in you in the middle of your suffering? Are there lies the enemy has paraded in the midst of your pain? It could be bitterness, loss of hope, mistrust, apathy, and a host of so many things. Ask the Lord to show you the schemes of the enemy in your suffering.

_____

_____

_____

COMMUNITY CONNECTION

1. Why do you think the enemy launches such a targeted onslaught on us in the midst of our suffering?

2. In your own suffering, where are each of you as individuals in the process? As you answer this, use the story of Mephibosheth as a metaphor to your relationship with God. Do you feel like you're: 1) outside of the kingdom; 2) at the table, amazed in receiving what is restored; or 3) in a place of simply wanting to be near the King even if suffering shows itself again?

3. Where does suffering seem too hard to bear in your own life? Are there specific examples that seem hopeless or too heavy to carry?

4. As a group, pray over one another in the places where suffering wants to overwhelm and keep you broken. Remind each other as you pray that the broken places can be restored and that the promise of eternity with God means the end to war, tears, sickness, and pain. Bear well with one another in the hard places and exhort one another in the coming reality of God making all things new.

Suffering is never wasted in the kingdom of God. It produces fruit that no other seed can generate. There is a start and an end to suffering, and Jesus, the author and perfector of your faith, will write the ending to your story so that it works out for good if you let him. How comforting to know the battle is already won and the final chapter has been written! The Scripture 1 Peter 5:10, "After you have suffered a little while," really is true. This verse ends with restoration—either now, in eternity, or at his return. He will finish the story having confirmed us, strengthened us, and established us. He will ultimately restore what was lost. This is our hope! We can fix our gaze there in the utmost pain and draw near to a good God who is well-acquainted with the depths of our grief.

17

PURPOSING GLORY

But we all, with unveiled face, beholding as in a mirror
the glory of the Lord, are being transformed into the same
image from glory to glory, just as by the Spirit of the Lord.
— 2 Corinthians 3:18, NKJV

As you know by now, my house sits on land that couldn't show all its inherent beauty with trash, decay, vines, and weeds overtaking it. Left like this, our land would struggle to survive, much less produce anything life-giving. Forget the lavender aroma in the breeze, the spring green of the field after a rain, or even how the stately magnolia is the landmark that provides a canopy of shade. If we did not maintain our property, it would never reach its potential. God made land to do more than just survive; he made it to flourish. In the same way:

> Followers of Jesus can't display God's
> glory when their sin, entanglements, wounds,
> and ungodly beliefs override the landscape
> of their hearts.

If we ignore the effects of these things, our hearts become overwhelmed, overrun, and naturally distant from God. If we merely survive and focus solely on the work of maintenance, without a vision of what could be in our lives, then even the most dutiful, well-intentioned worker will eventually give up. Or worse, we would cultivate land far away from God, bitterly toiling in vain.

Disillusioned, we might do the work, but not as a son or daughter—but as a hired hand with an impossible task.

There is something more to behold than just maintenance. Like walking through a botanical garden, we don't go just to see things neat and tidy; rather, we go to see flourishing plants and walkways lined with flowers in abundance. We go to be inspired and see the harvest on display. God created us with a longing for beauty beyond what we can imagine. We long for a vision that comes from God—the hope of glory. We long for that transformation where we will no longer look like ourselves; instead, we will reflect our Creator and mirror his grace, wisdom, and beauty too.

Working in our yard every season without a vision for the future would be completely pointless. Pulling weeds is hard work that makes space for new plants to bloom, for soil to be set right, and for the yard to be transformed into something better than what it was. But if we only look at the weeds or only pick up trash, there's little awe and wonder in that work. Glory is the point because glory is what we were made for. The reason farmland lies bare before the harvest, the reason the cold of winter makes the surprise of spring so sweet and why the seed must be buried in the ground before sprouting green and new—is all about the final glory to be revealed in the land.

GOD'S GLORY ON DISPLAY

Just like I want to see something beautiful on our land, I want pieces of glory that point to the Lord in our home too. So when we moved into our house years ago, we wanted to be intentional about the first thing our guests saw as they walked in the door. We thought long and hard about what kind of art should greet them. We like to intentionally pick art that has meaning to us and that can start a conversation. In fact, we keep walls bare until we find something meaningful to live on them. Once we find something, though, we love to quickly hang it up and admire it.

> *Glory is what we were made for.*

One such beauty is a painting hanging in our foyer entry of the burning bush from Moses's encounter with God in the Midian desert. We placed it prominently in the entryway of our home so when guests enter our home, they can see it and we can talk about it. It's acrylic and stunning, with shades of red and green with a desert backdrop. We commissioned this burning bush painting like this because 1) it was burning but not consumed; 2) it was where Moses turned to see God and realized he was on holy ground; and 3) it marked the place where Yahweh appointed Moses to lead the exodus. We love that he turned from what he was doing to look. And that when he looked, he knew it was holy.

This painting is dear to us, and I often walk by it and stare at it, marveling at its beauty and the message it represents. I enjoy stopping and looking and acknowledging the holy ground before I go flying to my next task. As I work at my desk, I will turn to gaze at the beauty of it, even from across two rooms. I find myself wanting to view it wherever I am throughout my day. It speaks of a first freedom for Moses, when he took the time to turn and look and be appointed to what he was made for. It is dear to me on so many levels. It is a work that I hope you will cherish now too as it graces the cover of this book.

I sometimes wonder, *What would have happened to Moses if he didn't stop and inquire? What if he didn't take off his shoes and acknowledge the holy ground?* Or worse, *What if he didn't recognize that God was speaking in a way that he had not previously encountered?* So many ways that God could have called Moses, but he used a bush on fire in a desert, ablaze with purpose and anointing.

As brilliant as the painting is, I find myself even more in awe of its artist. The painting is amazing, yes, but the artist took a biblical story and painted it perfectly for us. It matches our home, our taste, and it sets the atmosphere of our life and work. The artist had been a stranger to us before this painting, yet from only two email threads she produced this work we cherish. I cannot gaze at the painting without giving thanks for the artist in my heart. The painting would not exist without her talent and vision. The colors would not blend and move without her skilled eye and intuition. The painting exists in its grandeur because she painted it.

The glory of God is like that too. We seek snowcapped mountains to climb and orange-pink sunsets to watch because they point us toward the glory of the One who created them. We travel and hike and wait for those moments in nature because they propel us to the Creator. They are beautiful, yes, but only because of God's skilled eye and creative hand—and the fact that he has placed appreciation for his glory in our hearts. We are drawn to this beauty because of God's beauty. We search for it in search of him. Likewise:

> When we are filled with his glory,
> others can see him in us.

This is the antidote to pride for us: when others recognize that the landscape of our hearts only looks glorious because of the divine impartation of God's grace in our lives. What people most admire in someone who has a whole heart—a heart without a veil and fully given to God—is his glory displayed through them. There is freedom in a heart without bondage and room for life to bloom. The Spirit of God is not quenched in a whole heart; it has room to move and be on display. Glory has space to occupy in a heart fully offered to God.

AUTHENTIC GLORY

Friends, what if we all live in this way? Where our lives overflow with the glory of God to such measure that it compels others to worship him? To hunger after this deposit of glory for themselves? That they become aware, just as we are, that weeds, trash, vines, and decay must be steadily removed so that abundant life can bloom? Could this be the aroma of Christ we are supposed to carry? Is this the mature Christian life for which we were designed? If we are willing to cultivate what God gives us and be disciplined in caring for it, what emerges displays holy beauty that stretches beyond us and points to God.

Yet how many times have we settled for the world's display of glory? How many times have we fished for a compliment, positioned ourselves for recognition, drummed up some sort of caricature of who we really are—when what we long for is God's pure glory on display in us? We were made to carry it. He knows that we are not fully satisfied unless we do. Christ in us is what we seek. We can go looking to fill it in other places, but even the most public praising of our talents or our achievements will not satisfy our desire to see him on display in our lives. Those accolades will come up lacking without glory.

Many people give lip service to God's glory in sports arenas and in concert halls, claiming, "To God be the glory." But that statement is sometimes just a punctuation mark at the end of a sentence they wrote. We can say it for good measure or superstitious placating of God, but how quickly a person can fall and the glory looks tainted. Often God's glory isn't a glorious moment on a highlight reel, but longstanding and recognizable, formed over hidden years in a person's life. His glory is fashioned in the discipline of cultivating and the relationship that it births between himself and his child.

GLORY ON DISPLAY

The glory of God displayed in us is something we cannot produce on our own, and it should pour forth with such beauty and grace that we don't need to offer an empty acknowledgment of God. People will see the true glory and will feel it and know it. It won't feel distorted or cheaply paraded. It will naturally produce worship and thanksgiving to God and often bring salvation to those who witness it.

If you are concerned about being prideful in bearing his glory, holy confidence is very different from arrogance. Knowing that you are completely unable to be who you are without God's glory on display is humbling. It kicks pride to the curb. This should cause you to diligently and joyfully submit yourself to the Master Gardener, knowing what can be. It's not just about maintenance; God has a plan to make your life flourish if you let him.

Glory does not equate to fame or fortune, recognition or power. Those are worldly counterfeits of glory. Holy glory is often produced in those hidden acts of daily maintenance and in an obedient posture of the heart to make room for it there. We were made to be image bearers and glory reflectors. Our diligent maintenance in response to God's grace produces joy when we know that the end result is the glory of God on display. We receive and even choose back-breaking maintenance, intentional diligence, and yes, even suffering when we are confident of the end result. Seeing our lives in this process and the harvest that follows should motivate people to seek the Artist; it should propel them toward God. They should see God in who we are and in what we do.

> *We were made to be image bearers and glory reflectors.*

Several people who've come to our house have inquired about our burning bush painting. They want one too; they want to know who created it and what inspired it. That should be the same response as others observe the glory of God displayed in our lives. They should glance at us, but *go looking for* the Artist, seeking the same results for themselves.

There is nothing holier or more beautiful than God's glory. We were made to carry it—it is our calling and chief purpose. We crave it and long for the day when our lives and surroundings fully reflect it. So we should joyfully and diligently make space for his glory to reside. Removing the weeds, vines, trash, and decay from our landscape creates space for his glory to pour in.

When we quiet the noise of our flesh, our spirit has room to receive this glory. This is important work—and a joyous one. Rejoice in the work that propels you to glory.

PERSONAL PRAYER

1. I agree with John Piper when he says, "Defining the glory of God is impossible."[11] His glory is the weight of God's infinite and perfect wisdom, truth, holiness, and magnificent beauty. And even those words don't do it justice. As followers of Jesus, we are to manifest God's glory. Something in our words and deeds should point to someone other than us.

   As you enter prayer now, take account of your life and ask God to show you where you demonstrate his glory in order to recognize what God is cultivating in your life. Remember, the glory of God looks very different from the glory of people. These demonstrations of his glory may be hidden from the rest of the world. They may be positions of your heart, postures that you take during trial and suffering, or even small, unnoticed acts. It is likely an uncomfortable question to ask him! We aren't used to praying in this way. But if we ask him, he is gracious to show us what really matters and how to partner with him in it. This revelation is his work—we just often miss it. Ask him to reveal those places where you carry his glory and list them below.

   _____

   _____

   _____

2. Has the work of cultivating overshadowed the joy of creating space for his glory? Ask the Lord to show your truest emotion in your personal response to dealing with sin, wounding, entanglements, and ungodly beliefs. Have you become tired? Frustrated? Numb? Disillusioned? Does cultivating your heart seem like an impossible task, one that you will never finish?

Ask him to help you name your truest heart's response to the work of guarding your heart, putting sin to death, exchanging lies for truth, and other maintenance that you need to do. As you write your most honest response to the work of cultivating your heart, ask God to renew your joy in the process.

_____

_____

_____

3. Often our truest emotion in the cultivating process is not joy. Sadly, it feels like grief when we don't believe we can be transformed. We may believe it for other people, but deep down, we feel like an impossible case. We know the Scriptures say we can be transformed, but we wonder if we are an exception to that truth.

Ask God to "renew a right spirit" within you and to show what your life would look like if you were truly transformed (Ps. 51:10, ESV). Ask him to give you new eyes to gaze upon the call to glorify him. Often, we don't know the joy in the work because we haven't allowed ourselves to see what being a partaker and carrier of his glory actually looks like. If that's you, ask him to change your heart and show you what carrying glory means. Be still and wait on the Lord for any truths he gives in response to your doubt about your personal transformation *and* his truth about what your life could look like carrying his glory. Write down your impressions below.

_____

_____

_____

_____

_____

COMMUNITY CONNECTION

1. Within your group, honestly share with one another the places in your life where you have used the phrase "to God be the glory" as a punctuation when you knew deep down that it was really on your own strength. Share the places where you've "exchanged the glory of the immortal God for images resembling mortal man" (Rom. 1:23, ESV). These are situations where you gave God credit but knew that you moved in your own means and motives.

2. Share with one another the areas of intentional cultivation that feel hard and unrelenting, the places where "the work" swallows the joy of glory. This is where you feel that sin, entanglements, wounds, and ungodly beliefs require obedient work in your heart and rob the vision of being transformed into a carrier of glory.

3. Often the places of our intentional cultivation feel burdensome because we have not beheld God in the midst of them. I cannot possibly pull all of the weeds, untangle the vines, remove the trash, and protect against the rot all by myself. He wants to partner with us. We are to guard our "heart with all diligence" so that springs of life flow forth (Prov. 4:23, NASB). That full life is found in him, and he joins us in our diligence. Confess in your group any individual self-sufficiencies that might stand in your way of beholding the Lord and being transformed from glory to glory. Acknowledge your great need to behold him in the process.

4. Finally, share with one another the places in your personal communion this week where you allowed yourself to catch a fresh vision of how specific places in your life would look if they were flooded with glory. Encourage one another in prayer in those places where you long to imitate, reflect, and be filled with the glory of God.

Decide today as a community that you want to be partakers of the Lord's glory and that you will seek his glory in the joyful obedience of cultivating your heart with him. Make it a sincere declaration, like staking a claim in your life. Declare your desire to be vessels that display his glory. Give him permission to move anything out of your hearts that would hinder his glory from fully reigning and drawing others to Jesus. "To God be the glory" should be what others proclaim as they see the intentional cultivating of your hearts, which are near to God with joy abounding. The fruit from that process will be evident and immeasurably more than you could ask or imagine. Take these first freedoms and make them your lifestyle of tending your heart. The harvest will be beautiful.

CONCLUSION

As I pulled into my driveway one day recently, I was overcome by the beauty of our land—the hydrangeas in full bloom, the way the bridge crosses the creek into the tree line, the bright green grass without a weed in sight, and new fuchsia flowers sprouting by our front door. Beholding it was truly satisfying for me. But it wasn't always like that.

As I've alluded to, when we bought our home, weeds were everywhere, plants were overgrown and neglected, and the yard looked disheveled at best. Intentionally cultivating something beautiful took time. We purposefully pulled every weed and cut vines to make space for what was life-giving.

In the same way, as you have discovered, these first freedoms—your purposed work to cultivate a wholehearted prayer life that produces something beautiful—have begun to reveal their beauty. These initial steps set a foundation not only for continued growth, but a lifestyle of quickly drawing near to God that keeps your heart tended. These steps will allow you to make David's prayer your own: "Search me, God, and know my heart; test me and know my anxious thoughts. See if there is any offensive way in me, and lead me in the way everlasting" (Ps. 139:23–24). The way everlasting has life and joy, and tending your heart is a good work with promised fruit. Guarding your heart with all diligence (Prov. 4:23) is no longer drudgery but fulfilling, because you do so from a place of nearness to God. The most peaceful place for us is close to God, who delights in helping us take these steps toward a whole heart.

The material we covered in Part 1 always involves making *The Connection* with God, which involves those steps in drawing near to him as sons and daughters and learning to live a lifestyle of abiding. Tending to the heart at a distance from God is pointless. As you continue in first freedoms, make connecting to God your new normal, pausing to do so throughout your day. Carve out intentional

> *The most peaceful place for us is close to God.*

time to meet with him and abide daily with him before you move to other needs in your prayer life. You were made for this kind of communion, because communion is the antidote for whatever might rob your joy and purpose.

The tools from Part 2, *The Core*, are practical ways to deal with the anxious or offensive thoughts that distort God's truth in our lives and keep us in bondage. As a general discipline in your prayer life, check how you're doing with these core pieces on a regular basis and truly give God permission to "search you" to unlayer areas of wounding, sin, ungodly beliefs, and entanglements. The initial work can feel overwhelming, but over time it becomes a matter of simple maintenance in your partnership with God. Examine your heart like you would get your car serviced. You don't want anything unseen to cause major problems or accidents. Don't wait for things to break down, so address them with God before they become problematic. Guard your heart with these tools regularly and tend the places that threaten to rob your heart.

Finally, Part 3 is *The Culmination* of our first freedoms. It is only possible when the material of Parts 1 and 2 is firmly rooted in your life. Winning in spiritual warfare, exchanging burdens and crowns, navigating suffering, and then walking in holy authority with the glory of God as your primary motivation all become possible. These disciplines can be a challenge in the Christian journey for sure, but the connection (Part 1) and core (Part 2) pieces refine you to become more like Jesus as you navigate them. As a result, the culmination pieces (Part 3) produce the abundant life we all long for.

With all three parts of this book—*Connection*, *Core*, and *Culmination*— the goal is that they become your first instinct in walking intimately with God. While you can easily use these steps on a walk or sitting in traffic, you should partake of them with extended time before the Lord. My ultimate hope is that you and your church community would build Freedom Prayer teams to help others walk in these steps too, while allowing a safe place in prayer for people to deal with the issues that keep them bound.[12]

Freedom is contagious and often is the catalyst for an individual to walk abundantly with God. If we don't truly know we are his workmanship and if we aren't connected to him in loving relationship, then we can't walk in the good works prepared for us. We might attempt it, but the end result will be lacking and feel miserable. God's heart longs to have his sons and daughters walk in the fullness of what Jesus purchased for them. Experiencing freedom, which comes from nearness to God, and relationally tending to our hearts are essential for all other works to be fruitful.

> The bride of Christ must be spotless before she can be effective.

The world needs the church to look the way God intended her to look in order to behold his glory as he intended them to.

First freedoms are like those first, wobbly steps of a toddler. For those of us who start to wobble again, "going backwards" and relearning what we thought we had already mastered can feel silly to us as adults. But I encourage you to become like a child learning these steps: start again and get your footing steady. Those toddler steps lead to mature legs that can run with perseverance and finish the race strong and with purpose and joy. When the work feels hard—like cutting new paths with God—take heart in knowing that once those paths are cut, they clear the way for abiding communion. They are clear for our new life in which the glory of God is on display.

These first steps in freedom through an abiding prayer life will become natural as you continue in them. What was once unfamiliar will become a way of life that quickly supports maturity in the Christian journey. You will return to them again and again and receive intimacy with God in deeper layers as you do. They lead to true freedom. Do not despise the process. When you get discouraged, turn and look to the holy ground of God.

Remember how pivotal it is to stop and recall what God has for you in these first freedoms. I know the courage it takes to step in, and I am honored that you chose to cultivate your prayer life in this way. Blessings to you as you continue to walk in freedom near to God.

NOTES

1. George Abbott-Smith, *A Manual Greek Lexicon of the New Testament* 3rd ed. (London: T&T Clark, 1986), s.v. "reward."

2. James Strong, *Strong's Exhaustive Concordance of the Bible* (Nashville: Abingdon Press, 1890), s.v. "make."

3. Hudson Taylor, *Union and Communion* (CCEL, 1914), 12, https://www.ccel.org/ccel/t/taylor_jh/union/cache/union.pdf.

4. See Col. 2:13–15; Heb. 2:14; 1 John 3:8; Rom. 8:37–39; Luke 4:6; Rom. 5:12–14; 2 Cor. 4:3–4; Rev. 21:3–4; Eph. 1:7–10; Rev. 20:10.

5. *Strong's*, s.v. "stronghold."

6. Hab. 2:3; Ps. 37:12–13; Ps. 59:8; 1 Cor. 7:32.

7. Jim Putman and Chad Harrington, *The Revolutionary Disciple: Walking Humbly with Jesus in Every Area of Life* (Nashville: HIM Publications, 2021), 241–242.

8. Sinclair Ferguson, "What Is Discernment?" May 8, 2020, ligonier.org.

9. *The NAS New Testament Greek Lexicon*, s.v. *"balloœ,"* accessed June 10, 2021, https://biblestudytools.com/commentaries/ballo/html.

10. John Gill, *Gill's Exposition of the Bible*, s.v. "Revelation 4:10," accessed June 10, 2021, https://biblehub.com/commentaries/revelation/4.html.

11. John Piper, "What Is God's Glory?" July 22, 2014, accessed June 10, 2021, https://www.desiringgod.org/interviews/what-is-gods-glory--2desiringgod.org.

12. You can learn more about building a Freedom Prayer team at FreedomPrayer.org.

ABOUT THE AUTHOR

JENNIFER BARNETT is the executive director of Freedom Prayer, a non-profit ministry devoted to training and building prayer teams across the globe with tools for freedom. She has founded and equipped Freedom Prayer teams across the country and around the world. Passionate about the church and prayer, she speaks about, advocates for, and writes on knowing God, inner healing, and the Christian journey.